TEACH US TO PRAY

Teach Us to Pray

The Lord's Prayer in the Early Church and Today

Justo L. González

WILLIAM B. EERDMANS PUBLISHING COMPANY
GRAND RAPIDS, MICHIGAN

Wm. B. Eerdmans Publishing Co.
4035 Park East Court SE, Grand Rapids, Michigan 49546
www.eerdmans.com

Published 2020
Printed in the United States of America

26 25 24 23 22 21 20   1 2 3 4 5 6 7

ISBN 978-0-8028-7796-3

Library of Congress Cataloging-in-Publication Data

Names: González, Justo L., author.
Title: Teach us to pray : the Lord's prayer in the early church and today
   / Justo L. González.
Description: Grand Rapids, Michigan : William B. Eerdmans Publish-
   ing Co., 2020. | Includes bibliographical references and index. |
   Summary: "A meditation on the importance of the Lord's Prayer for
   contemporary Christian life, with insights drawn from the wisdom
   and experience of early Christians" — Provided by publisher.
Identifiers: LCCN 2019057933 | ISBN 9780802877963 (paperback)
Subjects: LCSH: Lord's prayer — Criticism, interpretation, etc. — His-
   tory — Early church, ca. 30-600. | Prayer — Christianity — History —
   Early church, ca. 30-600. | Lord's prayer — Meditations.
Classification: LCC BV230 .G596 2020 | DDC 226.9/606 — dc23
LC record available at https://lccn.loc.gov/2019057933

Contents

CONTENTS

vi

Introduction

Prayer is at the very heart of Christian life. It is through prayer that we communicate with God, and often it is also through prayer that God communicates with us. Prayer isn't only about speaking but also about listening, not only about asking but also about yielding, not only meditation but also praise, not only a practice but also a mystery, not only a devotion but also a ministry.

Therefore, it's not surprising that, when Jesus had once finished praying, his disciples said to him, "Lord, teach us to pray, as John taught his disciples." The answer that the Lord gave them is well known — "When you pray, say: 'Father, hallowed be your name. Your kingdom come. Give us each day our daily bread. And forgive us our sins, for we ourselves forgive everyone indebted to us. And do not bring us to the time of trial'" (Luke 11:2–4). The same prayer, with slightly different wording, appears in the Sermon on the Mount:

> Our Father in heaven, hallowed be your name. Your kingdom come. Your will be done, on earth as it is in heaven. Give us this day our daily bread. And forgive us our debts, as we also have forgiven our debtors. And do not bring us to the time of trial, but rescue us from the evil one. [For the kingdom and the power and the glory are yours forever. Amen.] (Matt. 6:9–13)

Possibly not more than two decades after Matthew and Luke wrote their Gospels, even before all of the New Testament was written, an anonymous Christian instructed that the following prayer should be said three times a day:

> You shall pray just as the Lord commanded it in his gospel: "Our heavenly Father, hallowed be your name. Let your kingdom come. Let your will be done on earth just as it is in heaven. Give us today the bread that we need. And forgive us our debt just as we forgive our debtors. Do not lead us into temptation, but deliver us from evil. For yours is the power and the glory forever.[1]

From that early date and to this day, this prayer has played an important role in the worship and devotion of Christians. It is often called the "Our Father" because of its opening words. Most commonly it is called the "Lord's Prayer" because it was the Lord Jesus who taught it. And also, particularly in older writings, it is called the "Dominical Prayer," meaning that it is the prayer taught by the Lord or *Dominus*.

Sadly, more recently some churches have stopped saying this prayer as frequently as it was said in the past, even though it still is an important element in the worship of other churches. Perhaps the main reason why it's not used as frequently as it could be is the fear that too often this prayer becomes simply a formula to be repeated without giving the words much thought. Thus, the same sentiment that leads many to reject the use of written prayers leads them also to set aside the Lord's Prayer in favor of more spontaneous prayers, arguing that these express our deepest feelings in a way that no written prayer — not even the one that the Lord taught us — will ever do. As a Latino Protestant, I can understand such feelings, for we all remember the time when, after confessing their sins to a priest, believers were ordered to recite "ten Our Fathers and five Hail Marys" — or the time when people mindlessly repeated the Lord's Prayer while they said the Rosary. Such practices led to the notion that any written prayer — even the one that the Lord taught his disciples — had to be rejected so that prayer could be more spontaneous.

This is not new. Apparently by the year 252 some Christians were expressing similar sentiments, for Cyprian, who was then the Bishop of Carthage and would soon die as a martyr, has left some words, probably written in response to similar objections, in which he stresses the unparalleled value of the Lord's Prayer:

> He who made us to live, taught us also to pray, with that same benignity, to wit, wherewith He has condescended to give and confer all things else; in order that while we speak to the Father in that prayer and supplication which the Son has taught us, we may be the more easily heard. Already He had foretold that the hour was coming "when the true worshippers should worship the Father in spirit and in truth"; and He thus fulfilled what He before promised, so that we who by His sanctification have received the Spirit and truth, may also by His teaching worship truly and spiritually. For what can be a more spiritual prayer than that which was given to us by Christ, by whom also the Holy Spirit was given to us? What praying to the Father can be more truthful than that which was delivered to us by the Son who is the Truth, out of His own mouth? So that to pray otherwise than He taught is not ignorance alone, but also sin. . . .
>
> Let us therefore, brethren beloved, pray as God our Teacher has taught us. It is a loving and friendly prayer to beseech God with His own words, to come up to His ears in the prayer of Christ. Let the Father acknowledge the words of His Son when we make our prayer, and let Him also who dwells within in our breast Himself dwell in our voice.[2]

And thirteen centuries later Martin Luther expressed a similar conviction:

> As has often been said, however, this is certainly the very best prayer that ever came to earth or that anyone would ever have thought up. Because God the Father composed it through His Son and placed it in His mouth, there is for us no doubt that it pleases Him immensely.[3]

In other words, when we pray the Lord's Prayer we are using words taught to us by none other than God!

Naturally, this doesn't mean that we can use this prayer like a magical formula to receive from God whatever we wish nor that there is any particular value in repeatedly mouthing it without even thinking about what we are saying. But it certainly does mean that this prayer is to serve as a guide for our entire life of prayer — and, as we shall see later on, also for the rest of our lives. This is why it's often called the Model Prayer: it is to serve as a model for all our prayers. It is a prayer that warns us when our petitions deviate from God's will. It is a prayer that also reminds us of things about which we often forget to pray. Taken as a model, this prayer reminds us that every time we bring a petition before God we must make sure that it follows the guidelines of this prayer.

As believers, we must take seriously Paul's concern when he says that "we do not know how to pray as we ought." According to Paul, in response to our ignorance we have been given the gift of the Spirit, for "that very Spirit intercedes with sighs too deep for words" (Rom. 8:26). From the earliest times and through the centuries, precisely because we share Paul's experience of not knowing exactly what to pray for, Christians have patterned their prayers after the one that Jesus himself taught his disciples. Thus, St. Augustine says,

No matter what else you say . . . [a]ll our words say nothing that
is not already included in the Lord's Prayer, if we indeed pray as
we ought. And anyone who says something that is not fitting to
this prayer in the Gospels, while praying lawfully, is still issuing
a carnal prayer.[4]

This fully agrees with what Thomas Aquinas would say more
than eight centuries later:

In the Lord's Prayer one not only asks for those things that ought
to be desired, but also does so in the order in which they ought
to be desired. Thus the Lord's prayer is not only a rule for our
petitions, but also a guide for all our sentiments.[5]

In the Greek-speaking East, several decades before the words of
Augustine quoted above, Gregory of Nyssa had already provided
an example of the manner in which this prayer is to serve as a model
for every prayer. He says,

By way of example, imagine that someone comes to God in
prayer but, not being aware of the unsurpassed greatness of the
one whom he is addressing, insults the divine majesty with petty
petitions. It is like the case of a person who is very poor and un-
educated and therefore thinks that earthen vessels are valuable.
If the king is offering great gifts and honors to his subjects, and
this person asks that the king put his hands into the clay and
make an earthen vessel, this would be an insult to the king. This
is precisely what happens when one prays without knowing what
one is doing, so that we do not rise up to the level of the giver,
but rather ask that God's power will come down to the level of
our earthly wishes.[6]

For this reason, I have two aims for this book. First, I will try to explain how the ancient church used and understood this prayer. I am convinced that what we learn in this regard will help us better understand not only the Lord's Prayer but also the gospel and all of life. My second purpose is, on the basis of what we learn from those ancient brothers and sisters, to share some reflections about the meaning of this prayer that the Lord taught us. I do this in the hope that such reflections will not only help you to understand more fully the words of the prayer but will also enrich and widen the scope of your life of prayer. With a view to these two purposes, I have structured this book by first explaining how the ancient church used this prayer that the Lord taught us and then, in later chapters, looking in more detail at each of its words and petitions, joining what we learn from those ancient Christians to our present-day experience. (Please note that all translations of early church texts, unless marked otherwise, are my own.)

However, perhaps the best way to express the purpose of this small book is to say that I have written it in a spirit of prayer and that I invite readers to read it in the same spirit. May we be guided in this endeavor by the Spirit who within our hearts cries, "Abba! Father!" (Gal. 4:6).

Uses of the Prayer
in the Early Church

The Wording of the Prayer

As we have seen, the Lord's Prayer has come to us in three slightly different versions — the ones in Matthew, Luke, and the *Didache* — most likely all dating from the first century. As early as the third century, Origen was already concerned about the different versions in the Gospels of Matthew and Luke. He concluded that the Lord had taught his disciples two different prayers on two different occasions. But this opinion was not generally accepted then, nor is it today. Throughout the centuries, as well as today, the general consensus has been that the two versions found in the Gospels are simply two different ways in which the same prayer was transmitted from one generation to another. The existence of a third version in the *Didache* seems to prove that, during the early decades of the life of the church, the prayer that the Lord taught his disciples was used fairly widely, although its oral rather than written use led to slightly different versions.

At any rate, from a very early date Matthew's version seems to have been the most widely used. Ancient Christian writers generally quote and study this version, and therefore we may conclude that this was also the version used in churches in the ancient world.

Private and Communal Hours of Prayer

The earliest extant witness to the use of this prayer in the ancient church is the passage quoted in the introduction from the first-century *Didache*, which directed believers to pray three times a day using this particular prayer. The *Didache* does not say whether believers would gather for prayer at three specific times, or they halted their activities for a moment of private prayer at those times, or they were simply encouraged to pray privately three times a day, but at no set hours. At that time, it was probably difficult for believers to gather three times a day, and therefore it seems that the *Didache* directs them to have three times of private prayer. However, the fact that the synagogue customarily had special times of prayer in the morning and evening, and sometimes also during the day, suggests that Christians would also follow that custom and gather at specific times to pray. Pliny the Younger confirmed the practice of at least some Christians to gather for morning prayer in a letter he wrote to Emperor Trajan reporting what he had learned from Christians who had been brought before him to be questioned. According to Pliny, some of these people declared that they had been Christians but were no longer, and they told him that "they used to gather at dawn in order to sing to Christ as to God and to covenant among themselves to abstain from all crime. . . . After this they would go their own ways, in order to gather again later to join in a meal."[1] This meal to which Pliny refers could be either Communion or a simple time of fellowship. Therefore, it appears that Christians would gather at least twice on the same day, first for morning prayer and then for this meal. The custom of having two specific hours of prayer, one in the morning and another at dusk, is confirmed by what Tertullian says late in the same century in his treatise *On Prayer*. There Tertullian suggests that believers pray at the third, sixth, and ninth hours — that is, approximately at nine in the morning, at noon, and at three in the afternoon. But then he adds that these prayers should take place "in addition to our regular prayers which are due, without any admonition, on the entrance of light and of night."[2] Still, here again it is unclear whether he meant these prayers to take place privately or as a gathered community.

Clearly, on all of these occasions the Lord's Prayer was at the heart of Christian prayer. In *On Prayer*, Tertullian affirms that it is permissible and perhaps even necessary to add to this prayer other petitions related more specifically to the circumstances and needs of those gathered but always following the guidance of the prayer that the Lord taught. Referring to the Lord's Prayer as "His Rule of Prayer," Tertullian says:

> Since, however, the Lord, the Foreseer of human necessities, said separately, after delivering His Rule of Prayer, "Ask, and ye shall receive"; and *since* there are petitions which are made according to the circumstances of each individual; our additional wants have the right — after beginning with the legitimate and customary prayers as a foundation, as it were — of rearing an outer superstructure of petitions, yet with remembrance of *the Master's* precepts.[3]

However, another, slightly later document sheds much light on the matter of the hours of prayer. This is the *Apostolic Tradition* of Hippolytus, which seems to have been written around the year 215, less than two decades after Tertullian's treatise on prayer. Hippolytus was rather conservative and wrote mostly to protest the changes that he saw and to reaffirm what he claimed had been the practice of Christians since the beginning of the apostolic tradition. Therefore, although the writing itself is slightly later than Tertullian's, it reflects practices already in use by Tertullian's time.

Among the many instructions that Hippolytus provides regard-

ing worship and various practices within the life of the church is
an extensive section on prayer and its appropriate times. This is a
passage that deserves extensive quotation:

> Let all the faithful, whether men or women, when early in the
> morning they rise from their sleep before they undertake any
> tasks, wash their hands and pray to God; and so they may go to
> their duties. But if any instruction in God's word is held [that day],
> everyone ought to attend it willingly, recollecting that he would
> hear God speaking through the instructor and that prayer in the
> church enables him to avoid the day's evil. . . .
>
> But if on any day there is no instruction, let everyone at home
> take the Bible and read sufficiently in passages he finds profitable.
>
> If at the third hour thou art at home, pray then and give thanks
> to God; but if thou chance to be abroad in that hour, make thy
> prayer to God in thy heart. For at that hour Christ was nailed to
> the tree. . . .
>
> At the sixth hour likewise pray also, for, after Christ was nailed
> into the wood of the cross, the day was divided and there was a
> great darkness. . . .
>
> And at the ninth hour let a great prayer and a great Thanks-
> giving be made. . . . At that hour, . . . Christ poured forth from his
> pierced side water and blood. . . .
>
> Pray again before thy body rests on thy bed.
>
> At midnight arise, wash thy hands with water and pray. And if
> thy wife is with thee pray ye both together. . . .
>
> It is needful to pray at this hour, for those very elders who gave
> us the tradition taught us that at this hour all creation rests for a
> certain moment, that all creatures may praise the Lord. . . .
>
> And at cockcrow rise up and pray likewise, for at that hour
> of cockcrow the children of Israel denied Christ, whom we have
> known by faith.[4]

These words make it clear that Hippolytus is dealing both with prayers that are to take place at home or during the day's business and with the prayers and times of study that take place in the community of the church. The prayers upon rising, on the third hour either at home or away from it, and before going to bed at night are sometimes held in private and sometimes in the company of other believers in the same household. But Hippolytus refers to other gatherings which offer, besides prayer, an opportunity for instruction and inspiration. Thus, we see here the beginning of the practice of setting aside certain times for private prayer as well as others for communal prayer. Hippolytus does not tell us on which of these occasions the Lord's Prayer was used nor how it related to other prayers. But we can suppose that what Tertullian and others had said earlier about basing all prayer on the Lord's Prayer still held as a basic principle in the practice of prayer, both private and communal.

The fourth century brought about profound changes in the Roman Empire and its relationship with the church. Early in the fourth century, Christianity suffered its worst persecution up to that time. Then in 313 Emperors Constantine and Licinius put an end to persecution. By 381, Christianity had become the official religion of the empire. Great churches were built, the monastic movement flourished, liturgy became more formal, bishops and other Christian leaders were respected, and Christian literature flourished. For good or for evil — or perhaps for both good and evil — the life of the church changed radically.

As a result of these changes, testimonies abound about Christian worship in the fourth century. On the basis of such testimonies, we learn that by then both morning and evening prayer had become community events — as they had been earlier in the synagogue. As to the other hours of prayer, various witnesses point in different directions.

Possibly the earliest of these witnesses is Eusebius of Caesarea, who, commenting on Psalm 90, says that "in the morning, we announce the mercy of God for us; and in the evening we point to his truth by means of a chaste and sober life." According to Eusebius, on such occasions churches throughout the world raise hymns and praise. Although this clearly shows that by this time there were certain prescribed hours for prayer, it is not clear whether this always took place in community or, at times, privately. A few decades later, Epiphanius of Salamis speaks of the practice of gathering both in the morning and in the evening in order to pray. Somewhat later John Chrysostom also refers to the same two hours of communal prayer, adding that at those times prayers are raised on behalf of the entire world, as well as for its rulers and others in authority — a subject to which we shall return later. The same is attested by Ambrose, Augustine, and several others.

One important text that illumines not only prayer but also much of Christian life in the Greek-speaking world during the second half of the fourth century is the *Diary* that Egeria sent to other women in her native Galicia (she calls them "sisters," which may well be a group of nuns or simply her siblings), telling them about her experiences in a long pilgrimage to the Holy Land. In that diary she offers a detailed description of the services that took place in Jerusalem. While her information is extremely valuable for the history of Christian worship in general, it also gives us a glimpse into the hours of prayer as they were followed in Jerusalem. According to Egeria, all the doors of the Church of the Resurrection were opened every morning before the crow of the cock. (It is interesting to note that what among Greek-speakers in Jerusalem was called the Church of the Resurrection — the *Anastasis* — in the Latin-speaking West was called the Holy Sepulcher. These two names for the same place illustrate the Western tendency to stress the cross and death of Jesus over his resurrection.) The first to enter the church were the monks and the "virgins" — that is, nuns — as well as any laymen or laywomen who wished to rise at such an early hour. They would then sing psalms and antiphons, interspersed with prayers led by deacons and presbyters, until sunrise. At sunrise the bishop and his entourage would enter, go directly to the very place of the resurrection, and there lead a long prayer. Something similar happened at noon, and then again at three in the afternoon, when people gathered once again at the same place and were again led in prayer by the bishop. The early afternoon prayers at three o'clock were followed at four o'clock by the service of illumination, when all the lamps and candles were lit for the evening. On Sundays, however, in celebration of the resurrection, all the lights were already lit by the time of the early morning service.

We don't know to what degree the practices in Jerusalem were mirrored in other areas. We do know that, although the hours and ceremonies may not have been the same, the practice had long been developing to set aside certain times for prayer and to make attendance at such services the particular responsibility of monastics. Egeria repeatedly refers to the participation of monks and virgins (nuns) in these hours of prayer. She also says that the people who were not monastics were not required to be present for such prayers but were free to participate or not as they wished. Partly as a result of the great changes that began under the rule of Constantine, monastics — men as well as women — continued keeping the ancient hours of prayer and even expanding them, while other people came to believe that the task of praying and interceding for the rest of the world was now entrusted solely to monastics.

While this was happening in churches in cities and towns, a similar process was taking place within the monastic community. From its very beginning cenobitic monasticism — that is, monastic life in community rather than in the solitude practiced by hermits — included set hours of prayer. Pacomius, often considered

13

the founder of cenobitic monasticism, dictated that his monasteries would have three particular times set aside for prayer during the day and a fourth during the night. Soon other hours were added to these. A few decades after Egeria's pilgrimage, John Cassian brought to the West what he had seen of monastic life in Egypt and Palestine. In his *Institutions*, Cassian speaks of seven times for prayer and, in order to bolster prayers at the third, sixth, and ninth hours, made use of the same Scripture passages already mentioned to refer to important events that took place at each of these hours. Furthermore, as proof that setting aside seven times, or hours, of prayer reflects the will of God, he quotes Psalm 119:164: "Seven times a day I praise you for your righteous ordinances."

Although this takes us beyond our focus on the history of early prayer, the practice of setting aside particular times for prayer became a mark of monastic life. In the West uniformity in these practices grew, thanks to the Rule of St. Benedict, which says,

> As the prophet says, "Seven times a day I praised you." We shall fulfill this sacred sevenfold number if we meet our obligations in the hours of Matins, Prime, Terce, Sext, None, Vespers, and Compline. It is about these daily hours that the prophet said, "Seven times a day I praised you." The same prophet also said of the night prayers, "I would rise in the middle of the night to confess you." Therefore, at these times let us praise our creator for the judgments of his justice: Matins, Prime, Terce, Sext, None, Vespers, and Compline. And let us also rise at night to confess him.[5]

The Lord's Prayer, Catechesis, Baptism, and Communion

From the earliest times, baptism, Communion, and the Lord's Prayer have been connected. The prayer in the eighth chapter of the *Didache*, which has already been quoted, appears between chapter 7, which is about baptism, and chapter 9, which is about Communion. Many of the ancient texts referring to the Lord's Prayer occur within the context of preparation for baptism. Tertullian's treatise *On Prayer* has all the signs of having been written to prepare catechumens for baptism. The same is true of Cyprian's treatise on the Lord's Prayer. It was customary in the ancient church for anyone requesting baptism to go through a period of catechumenate, or religious instruction, that normally lasted at least two years. At the end of that time the catechumen was taught the symbol, or creed, to affirm at baptism, and the Lord's Prayer was explained. For this reason, much of what we now find regarding the Lord's Prayer in documents from the early church is set in a context of preparation for baptism.

The *Catechetical Lectures* of Cyril of Jerusalem, delivered during Lent in 350, provide a clear example of this connection. Since it was customary for most baptisms to take place on Easter Sunday, during the last weeks before that great celebration, that is, during what we now call Lent, bishops had to make sure that those who were preparing to receive baptism understood the basic tenets of Christianity and lived as Christians. The *Catechetical Lectures* of Cyril are a series of twenty-three talks in which he addresses candidates for baptism in his church. As he nears the end of the last of these lectures, Cyril explains to his audience the order and meaning of Communion, of which they have not yet been able to partake. When his narrative comes to the moment in Communion that the Lord's Prayer will be said, Cyril offers a detailed exposition of the meaning of that prayer — an exposition to which we shall return later in this book.

Another equally clear example of the prayer's connection to baptism appears in Augustine's sermon number 57, which is described as "bequeathing the prayer [of the Lord] after the Symbol [the Creed] to the *competentes* [the name that was given to those about to be baptized]." Addressing these *competentes*, Augustine tells them that "your spiritual formation follows an order in which you must first learn what you are to believe, and then you learn what you are to ask for."[6] This reflects the custom of gathering those about to be baptized to be taught both the creed and the Lord's Prayer under the leadership of the bishop. Augustine is simply saying that his audience has already learned the creed they will have to affirm at their baptism, and he is now about to explain to them the Lord's Prayer.

Thus, all would seem to indicate, on the one hand, that learning the Lord's Prayer was one of the basic elements in preparation for baptism. But, on the other hand, if taken literally, this would seem to mean also that candidates for baptism had not heard or learned this prayer until the final days of their preparation for baptism. However, we know that this was not the case, for the Lord's Prayer was at the very center of the communal prayers of the church — particularly morning and evening prayer — in which both those who had already been baptized and those who were still seeking baptism were expected to participate. Thus, we may surmise that, while the catechumens did hear and repeat the Lord's Prayer at various times, the prayer was not fully explained to them until they were about to be baptized.

The Wider Significance of the Lord's Prayer

Having summarized what we know about the use of the Lord's Prayer in the life and devotions of the ancient church, I wish to stress that the documents we have make it clear that for those early Christians this prayer was much more than a few words to be repeated or a magic formula to be included in the rites of the church and in individual devotions. The Lord's Prayer served as a summary of Christian life and as a measure by which to judge all that was asked of God, as well as of all one did. In North Africa, which for several centuries was the center of Latin Christian theology, Tertullian said that this prayer is as diffuse in meaning as it is compressed in words. For it has embraced not only the special duties of prayer, be it veneration of God or petition for man, but almost every discourse of the Lord, every record of *His* Discipline; so that, in fact, in the Prayer is comprised an epitome of the whole Gospel.[7]

A few decades later, still in North Africa, Cyprian also declared,

But what matters of deep moment are contained in the Lord's Prayer! How many and how great, briefly collected in the words, but spiritually abundant in virtue! so that there is absolutely nothing passed over that is not comprehended in these our prayers and petitions, as in a compendium of heavenly doctrine.[8]

Likewise, but now in Alexandria, Origen spoke of the wide scope and great value of this prayer: "Let us not imagine that what we have learned is just some words that we are to repeat at certain times set aside for prayer. . . . Our entire life is to be a constant prayer that says 'Our Father, who art in heaven.'"[9]

Summary

Take note of four points as we conclude this chapter. First of all, in the early years of the life of the church, its members, still mostly Jews, continued to follow the hours of public and private prayer that were part of the tradition of the synagogue. Some time later, other hours of prayer were added: the third, sixth, and ninth hours of the day. Generally, the only periods of community prayer were those that took place at dusk and dawn — evening and morning prayer. Even these were not required of all believers but only of those who could and would participate. As a result of the changes that began during the time of Constantine, attendance at the set hours of prayer became more and more the sole responsibility of monastics, and general attendance by the rest of the church declined for these hours.

Second, the Lord's Prayer was the foundation for all communal prayers and was expected to be also at the heart of private devotions. This meant, on the one hand, that periods of communal prayer should include it. But it also meant, on the other hand, that this prayer was to be used as a model for what, how, and to whom one is to pray in private devotions. Repeating it is a way of ensuring that all other prayers and petitions are proper.

Third, we have seen that the Lord's Prayer was closely associated with baptism and Communion. Because baptism is a new birth, we can address God as Father. Later we will also note that quite frequently those early Christians saw a relationship between the daily bread for which they asked in the Lord's Prayer and the bread of life of which they partook in Communion.

Finally, this prayer was important not only because it was to be repeated at various times and in certain circumstances and because all petitions and prayers must follow its guidelines, but also because the prayer itself would shape the entire life of those who repeatedly and sincerely pray "Our Father."

Let us now turn to the study of the prayer itself.

I

Our Father who art in heaven, hallowed be
thy name. Thy kingdom come. Thy will
be done on earth as it is in heaven. Give us
this day our daily bread. And forgive us our
debts, as we forgive our debtors. Lead us not
into temptation. But deliver us from evil.
For thine is the kingdom, and the power,
and the glory forever. Amen.

Beginning with "Our Father"

Although the first word of the Lord's Prayer in English is *Our*, this is not the case in the original. Because of grammatical differences between English and Greek, in English we say "Our Father" but in Greek the word order is reversed: "Father Our" — *Patēr hēmōn*. Therefore, although in this chapter we begin with the first word in the English version, we should be aware that before saying "our" many Christians today begin by saying "Father." This was also true of early Christians who spoke and prayed in either Greek or Latin.

A Personal Experience

It was some sixty years ago. I was opening the day with private prayer at the small prayer chapel of the seminary where I was studying in Matanzas, Cuba. In my devotions, as I very often did, I turned to the Lord's Prayer and began saying "Our Father. . . ." But then I realized that I was by myself. Why should I say "Our Father" rather than "My Father"? When I said "our," didn't this show that I was simply repeating the prayer without thinking about it?

Being alone, shouldn't I address God as "*my* Father" rather than as "our Father"?

This brought another thought to mind. Could it be that, even though at that point I was physically alone, I was not addressing God on my account only but also in the name of my wider community? So then I thought that the word *our* with which I was addressing God included the rest of the seminary community. I knew that at that time some of my classmates were also praying; therefore, it was quite natural to think that when I said "Our Father," I was speaking also on behalf of my classmates, my teachers, the groundskeeper, and the president's secretary. All of us together were "we." But then that "we" whose prayer I was joining grew further and further. "We" included also the congregation with whom I regularly worshipped. It included not only that congregation, but many other churches like mine. And not only those churches, but also many others in far-away lands where millions of people were also saying "Our Father." Even though we did not know or even think about it, we were all together addressing God as our common parent. And, couldn't it also be true that when I said "Our," I was joining believers even beyond those who were then seeking to be faithful to the gospel but also many others who had already departed to the Lord? I was joining not only my seminary community, and not only my contemporaries throughout the world, but even the many generations who in years and centuries past had prayed "Our Father." The "we" with whom I was praying included Augustine and Monica, Macrina and Basil, as well as an innumerable multitude of sisters and brothers whose names I did not know but are written in the book of life.

Thus, when we say "Our Father," we are not praying alone, even when we pray in private. In hundreds of different languages, in tall-steepled churches and in small chapels with thatched roofs, privately and in the midst of multitudes, this great "we" who are the body of Christ raise our unanimous prayer: "Our Father."

Ancient Witnesses

What I discovered in that small prayer chapel has been known by many Christians from ancient times. Cyprian, the Bishop of Carthage in North Africa, wrote,

> Before all things, the Teacher of peace and the Master of unity would not have prayer to be made singly and individually, as by one who prays to pray for himself alone. For we say not "My Father, which art in heaven," nor "Give me this day my daily bread"; nor does each one ask that only his own debt should be forgiven him; nor does he request for himself alone that he may not be led into temptation, and delivered from evil. Our prayer is public and common; and when we pray, we pray not for one, but for the whole people, because we the whole people are one. The God of peace and the Teacher of concord, who taught unity, willed that one should thus pray for all, even as He Himself bore us all in one.[1]

In the next century Theodore of Mopsuestia, one of the greatest biblical scholars of antiquity, declared,

> I do not wish you to say *my Father* but *our Father*, because He is a Father common to all in the same way as His grace, from which we received adoption as sons, is common to all. In this way you should not only offer congruous things to God, but you should also possess and keep fellowship with one another, because you are brothers and under the hand of one Father.[2]

And John Chrysostom, considered the most eloquent preacher of all ages, expressed this quite clearly, while also suggesting that the common paternity of God that Christians share also has radical consequences for the ordering of society:

He [Jesus] teaches, moreover, to make our prayer common, in behalf of our brethren also. For He saith not, "my Father, which art in Heaven," but, "our Father," offering up his supplications for the body in common, and nowhere looking to his own, but everywhere to his neighbor's good. And by this He at once takes away hatred, and quells pride, and casts out envy, and brings in the mother of all good things, even charity, and exterminates the inequality of human things, and shows how far the equality reaches between the king and the poor man, if at least in those things which are greatest and most indispensable, we are all of us fellows. For what harm comes of our kindred below, when in that which is on high we are all of us knit together, and no one hath aught more than another; neither the rich more than the poor, nor the master than the servant, neither the ruler than the subject, nor the king than the common soldier, nor the philosopher than the barbarian, nor the skillful than the unlearned? For to all hath He given one nobility, having vouchsafed to be called the Father of all alike.[3]

Chrysostom earned the virulent hatred of many among the powerful when, at the Cathedral of St. Sophia in the imperial capital, he dared follow this understanding of the gospel to its consequences, declaring that the enormous differences between the rich and the poor and between the ruling classes and the rest of the population were incompatible with the gospel itself. Eventually this would lead first to his exile and then to death. Clearly, one reason that Chrysostom suffered this fate was his conviction that, since all pray to a common Father, all are obliged to treat one another as brothers and sisters.

Intercessory Prayer

This *we* that is implied when we say "our Father" may well reach beyond the limits of those who raise this prayer. From the early documents of Christianity we learn that the followers of Jesus were not supposed to pray only for themselves but rather to intercede far more widely. As 1 Timothy shows, this is grounded on the very character of God and God's relationship with humanity:

> First of all, then, I urge that supplications, prayers, intercessions, and thanksgivings be made for everyone, for kings and all who are in high positions, so that we may lead a quiet and peaceable life in all godliness and dignity. This is right and is acceptable in the sight of God our Savior, who desires everyone to be saved and to come to the knowledge of the truth. For there is one God; there is also one mediator between God and humankind, Christ Jesus, himself human, who gave himself a ransom for all. (1 Tim. 2:1–6a)

. While these words point to the need to practice intercessory prayer, they don't refer to a particular occasion but rather to the entire prayer life of believers, both in private and as a community. However, as the church began to pay particular attention to the task of believers to pray for one another as well as for the rest of humankind, this became part of the worship service. We know that at least as early as the second century, Christian worship included both the service of the word and the service of the table. The first of these was open to all, baptized or not. In this service of the word, amid various prayers and hymns, much time was devoted to studying the word of God. In order to understand the importance of this first part of a full worship service, we must remember that at that time it was not possible for all believers to have their own Bibles and read them privately in their homes. Therefore, the only opportunity that many had to hear the reading of Scripture and its explanation was the service of the word. At the end of the service of the word, those who would not partake in the service of the table — Communion — were dismissed. Those who left at this point included both those who had not yet made a decision to become Christians and those who had made that decision and were preparing for baptism. People in this second group were called *catechumens*, and their time of preparation for baptism would often be two years or more. After the dismissal of those who would not partake of Communion, those who remained took part in the prayer of the faithful, followed by the kiss of peace. One of the earliest witnesses that we have on these matters comes from Justin, who died as a martyr in the mid-second century. He says,

> But we, after we have thus washed him who has been convinced and has assented to our teaching, bring him to the place where those who are called brethren are assembled, in order that we may offer hearty prayers in common for ourselves and for the baptized [illuminated] person, and for all others in every place, that we may be counted worthy, now that we have learned the truth, by our works also to be found good citizens and keepers of the commandments, so that we may be saved with an everlasting salvation. Having ended the prayers, we salute one another with a kiss.[4]

Hippolytus also refers to the prayers of the faithful in his *Apostolic Tradition*. After discussing in some detail how people are to be prepared for baptism and how this is to be administered and then moving into the service of the table, Hippolytus says, "Now let them [the recently baptized] pray with the people. But they are not to pray with the people before all the precedent has been done. Once they have prayed, let them offer the kiss of peace."[5] The instruction that those who had not yet been baptized were not to pray with the faithful requires some explanation. We know that that those who were preparing for baptism took part in many of the prayer occasions that have already been discussed. In the same writing, slightly earlier, when he is explaining the process of preparation for catechumens, Hippolytus says that they are to pray by themselves, apart from believers. This means that the unbaptized were certainly allowed and encouraged to pray. They were expected to attend meetings for biblical, moral, and doctrinal instruction; and there is no doubt that prayers were offered in such meetings. What Hippolytus forbids — and Justin seems to say the same — is those who are not yet baptized being part of a special prayer that is raised almost immediately before Communion, as part of the service of the table. This prayer, which eventually came to be called the prayer of the faithful, the great intercession, or the universal prayer, was part of the mission of the church as a priestly body, and this meant that only those who through baptism had become members of that priestly body could take part in it.

The rite of anointing a person during baptism pointed to this idea of priesthood. In the Old Testament, people were usually anointed in order to fulfill the roles of priests and kings. For instance, in Exodus 13:30 and 40:13, Aaron and his sons are anointed as priests; and the two books of Samuel include many references to the anointing of Saul and David. Thus, the anointing of those who had just been baptized was an indication that now they were part of the royal priesthood of the church.

Biblical Background

The ancient church understood itself as a priestly people and therefore as a fulfillment of the promise made earlier to Israel when God said to them, "You shall be for me a priestly kingdom and a holy nation" (Exod. 19:6). In the New Testament we have the well-known words in 1 Peter, whose readers are told that they are "a royal priesthood, a holy nation" (1 Pet. 2:9). Also, almost at the very beginning of the book of Revelation we read that Jesus Christ, who is "the ruler of the kings of the earth," is also the one who "made us to be a kingdom, priests serving his God and Father" (Rev. 1:5–6). Later in the same book we find a hymn praising God's work in believers, making them "a kingdom and priests serving our God" (Rev. 5:10), and almost at the end of the book we read that believers "will be priests of God and of Christ, and they will reign with him a thousand years" (Rev. 20:6). The main role of a priest is to take the people before the presence of God. Likewise, the role of the church as a priestly body is to take one another before that presence, each serving as a priest for the rest, and all jointly taking the entire creation before the heavenly throne.

Given this understanding, it is clear that this task of praying for the rest of the world was not simply an invitation for each individual to do so or even the obligation of that individual to intercede for humankind, but it was also and above all a task of the entire church as a single body. Thus, although any believer could partake in the daily prayers at the established hours and could also pray during the service of the word on Sunday, only those who had been brought into the priestly body of the church through baptism were allowed to take part in the great priestly prayer of the faithful.

The Universal Priesthood of Believers

A few years ago, as we prepared to commemorate the five-hundredth centennial of the Protestant Reformation, we constantly heard about the main tenets of that movement — the authority of Scripture, salvation by faith, the holiness of daily life, and so forth. One of the principles often mentioned in that context was the "priesthood of all believers," one of the main emphases of the Reformation. Not only did we study this in school, but we also heard it in church for many years because this was a frequent emphasis of Protestants in their polemics against Roman Catholicism. I remember the times when, as a young man in a predominantly Catholic country, one of

my favorite pastimes was to begin a discussion with a priest to let
him know in no uncertain terms that I no longer had any need of
him in order to approach God. I also remember that back then, in
my attempts to evangelize my classmates, I would tell them that it
was not necessary to have priests in order to approach God because
each of us could be our own priest and directly approach the throne
of the Most High. In a society like Cuba, in which there were strong
anticlerical feelings, this was a very effective argument.

Now, many years later, I realize that I did not have a proper
understanding of the priesthood of all believers. A more careful
reading of Luther, Calvin, and the other reformers shows that what
they were doing was not simply announcing that Scripture opposed
the idea that the church had need of a priesthood, but they were
also returning to the most ancient Christian literature and there
rediscovering the very notion of universal priesthood. I also know
now that this universal priesthood of believers has dimensions that,
at that time, I did not even suspect but which are of crucial importance for the life of the church as well as for its relationship with the
world in which it exists.

In a word, as I understood universal priesthood back then, it
simply meant that one did not need priests, for each of us was his
or her own priest. This had a certain value as a polemical point in
our conflicts with Roman Catholicism, but it is a very abridged and
impoverished understanding of universal priesthood. The priesthood of all believers does not mean simply or even first of all that
each of us is our own priest, but it means, above all, that we are all
priests for everyone else.

The difference between these two ways of understanding the
matter is fundamental. What I learned and repeated as a young man
bore the stamp of the harsh individualism that had taken hold of
Western culture, particularly in the nineteenth century, and that
still has a strong grasp on our thinking and our society. If each is his

or her own priest, this ultimately means that we do not need one another. It is not only the ordained priest who becomes dispensable but also the brother or sister who sits by us in church. The church, instead of being a single body whose head is Jesus Christ and whose members, in order to participate in the life of their head, have to be grafted into the body, becomes an agglomeration of individuals, each of us approaching God directly with no need for the others. This is why one frequently hears someone say, "I am a Christian after my own fashion, and I have no need for the church." It is also the reason why some believers go from church to church just as easily as they change a shirt. They look for another church because they did not like what brother so-and-so said, or because that other pastor is a better preacher, or because they prefer the music in a different church, or for whatever equally unimportant reason. This is also why many of our churches are divided, because some prefer one sort of worship and others a different form, forgetting that when we are joined in worship we are not worshiping only for ourselves but also for the rest. When, either in private or in the midst of the community, we repeat the prayer that the Lord taught us, we don't say "My Father" but rather "Our Father." We are praying in the name of a reality that is much wider than any one of us. When we worship we acclaim God in the name of all creation, just as when we pray to this Father of ours we do so representing a much wider body of which we are members. This is why one of the most ancient Christian hymns, which many today still repeat at Communion, says, "Therefore with angels and archangels, and with all the company of heaven, we laud and magnify your glorious name."

The universal priesthood of believers does not mean that each one serves as one's own priest, but rather that each one is a priest for all the others, and that all believers together are a priesthood for the entire world — which includes the world that does not believe, or pray, or even seek God. When understood thus, the universal priesthood, instead of making us individuals separately seeking our paths to God, joins us in a common ministry in which we approach God no longer as individual priests but rather as a priestly people. Our priesthood is not a private line to communicate with God without needing anyone else. It is rather a network in which we can count on the rest as priests for each of us, and where each is a priest for all the rest.

In short, when we say "Our Father," this *we* is not simply each of us separately. When, either privately or in the midst of the community of faith, I say "Our Father," I am not praying only for myself but also for the entire church that throughout the earth also calls the same God Father. Also, since the church is a priestly people whose mission is to pray for all of God's creation, the *we* in whose name we pray includes even those who do not pray because they do not believe. We intercede for them before God, asking for them all that we ask for ourselves.

Let us then pray for those who do not pray because they do not know the heavenly Father:

> **Our** Father who art in heaven, hallowed be thy name. Thy kingdom come. Thy will be done on earth as it is in heaven. Give us this day our daily bread. And forgive us our debts, as we forgive our debtors. Lead us not into temptation. But deliver us from evil. For thine is the kingdom, and the power, and the glory forever. Amen.

2

Our **Father** who art in heaven, hallowed be thy name. Thy kingdom come. Thy will be done on earth as it is in heaven. Give us this day our daily bread. And forgive us our debts, as we forgive our debtors. Lead us not into temptation. But deliver us from evil. For thine is the kingdom, and the power, and the glory forever. Amen.

A Welcome Surprise

Father. Reading the ancient commentaries and sermons on the Lord's Prayer, we see that much of the attention of those early Christians is centered on this particular word. Today, partly for the same reasons but also for new ones, this word in the Lord's Prayer is again the most discussed and one that, in certain circles, creates the most difficulties.

In the case of those ancient Christian writers, calling God "Father" was particularly important for what it says about the relationship between God and believers. Unfortunately, another reason this word was important for them was that the title of God as the "Father" was often used to attack Judaism, for early Christians wrongly claimed that seeing God as a father was an idea totally alien to Judaism. For instance, Cyprian claims that because the Jews have not accepted Jesus they are no longer children of God:

> A word this [Father], moreover, which rebukes and condemns the Jews, who not only unbelievingly despised Christ, who had been announced to them by the prophets, and sent first to them, but

also cruelly put Him to death; and these cannot now call God
their Father, since the Lord confounds and confutes them, saying,
"Ye are born of your father the devil, and the lusts of your father
ye will do. For he was a murderer from the beginning, and abode
not in the truth, because there is no truth in him." And by Isaiah
the prophet God cries in wrath, "I have begotten and brought up
children; but they have despised me. The ox knoweth his owner,
and the ass his master's crib; but Israel hath not known me, and
my people hath not understood me. Ah sinful nation, a people
laden with sins, a wicked seed, corrupt children! Ye have forsaken
the Lord; ye have provoked the Holy One of Israel to anger." In
repudiation of these, we Christians, when we pray, say Our Father;
because He has begun to be ours, and has ceased to be the Father
of the Jews, who have forsaken Him. Nor can a sinful people be a
son; but the name of sons is attributed to those to whom remission
of sins is granted, and to them immortality is promised anew, in
the words of our Lord Himself: "Whosoever committeth sin is the
servant of sin. And the servant abideth not in the house for ever,
but the son abideth ever."[1]

Somewhat more moderate, but still rather prejudiced, are the
words of Augustine. While claiming that "nowhere can one find
any precepts ordering the people of Israel to say 'Our Father,' or
that they should pray to God as father," Augustine affirms that "the
prophets repeatedly show that the same Lord of ours could also be
their Father if they would keep his commandments."[2]

However, even though they often use the name Father to attack
Judaism, what was most important for ancient Christians about
calling God "Father" was what it meant regarding the relationship
between God and believers. Both of these elements may be seen in
the following words of Tertullian:

The prayer begins with a testimony to God, and with the reward of faith, when we say, "Our Father who art in the heavens"; for (in so saying) we at once pray to God, and commend faith, whose reward this appellation is. It is written, "To them who believed on Him He gave power to be called sons of God." However, our Lord very frequently proclaimed God as a Father to us; nay, even gave a precept that we call no one on earth father, but the Father whom we have in the heavens: and so, in thus praying, we are likewise obeying the precept. Happy they who recognize their Father! This is the reproach that is brought against Israel, to which the Spirit attests heaven and earth, saying, "I have begotten sons, and they have not recognized me." Moreover, in saying "Father," we also call Him "God." That appellation is one both of filial duty and of power. Again, in the Father the Son is invoked; "for I," saith He, "and the Father are One."[3]

(In passing, note that further on in this passage Tertullian proves to be a precursor of Cyprian's famous dictum that "it is impossible to have God as Father without having the church as mother." Tertullian says that "nor is even our mother the Church passed by, if, that is, in the Father and the Son is recognized the mother, from whom arises the name both of Father and of Son."[4])

Probably most outstanding in the various writings of the time, however, is a prevailing note of surprise at the possibility of being invited to call God "Father." Thus, Cyprian expresses the importance of this title as a sign of the unexpected grace of God:

But how great is the Lord's indulgence! how great His condescension and plenteousness of goodness towards us, seeing that He has wished us to pray in the sight of God in such a way as to call God Father, and to call ourselves sons of God, even as Christ is the Son of God, — a name which none of us would dare to venture on in prayer, unless He Himself had allowed us thus to pray![5]

In his treatise *On the Sacraments*, Ambrose of Milan also stresses the significance of being able to call God "our Father," but he also notes the dangers involved in the improper use of this title:

> It is not inappropriate pride to glory in what you have received. It is rather a sign of true filial love. Lift up your eyes to the Father who gave you birth through baptism and redeemed you through his Son. Call him: "Our Father!" Even though this might seem an unwarranted pride, it is holy. But at the same time you must beware of the danger of overcoming its limits. When you call God "Father" as a child does, do not think that this is a privilege that you have above others. Only Christ can claim God as his Father in that privileged sense. The rest of us have him as Father jointly. Christ was begotten by God, while we on the other hand were created.[6]

What makes this feeling of surprise even greater is the appellative *Abba*, which was the equivalent of "*my* Father," and which was frequently used in the church to address God, as we see in the New Testament (see Mark 14:36; Rom. 8:15; Gal. 4:6). This is one of the few Aramaic words that the church continued using even as Gentiles began to outnumber Jews in the church.

Radical Consequences

The very use of this appellative to address God has radical consequences. Both Tertullian and Cyprian connected the opening words of this prayer with the commandment of Jesus not to call anyone on earth father, but only God in heaven. Referring to the practice of repeating the Lord's Prayer immediately after baptism, Cyprian declares that the words themselves are witness to the neophyte's radical decision to follow only the heavenly Father and not an earthly one. He says,

> The man, therefore, who has believed in His name, and has become God's son, ought from this point to begin both to give thanks and to profess himself God's son, by declaring that God is his Father in heaven; and also to bear witness, among the very first words of his new birth, that he has renounced an earthly and carnal father, and that he has begun to know as well as to have as a father Him only who is in heaven.[7]

Harsh as this may seem, it was absolutely necessary in a society in which most parents probably were not supportive when their children decided to request baptism. If the new believer's father was the *paterfamilias* — that is, the head of the entire extended family — it was obligatory to obey him in all things, including matters of religion. Therefore, saying "Our Father" upon emerging from the waters of baptism would reaffirm the decision to join the church and follow the path of Jesus, even if it was against an earthly father's will.

This one word at the beginning of the Lord's Prayer — actually, the first word in the original Greek and in many other languages — has far-reaching consequences not only for the manner in which we conceive of God, but also for how we understand our own identity and for how we behave throughout life. Origen, the famous Alexandrian teacher of the late second and the early third centuries, declared that anyone who does not behave as a legitimate child of the Father sins grievously in using this prayer, for it adds blasphemy to the person's sins.[8] Gregory of Nyssa, slightly more than a century later, agreed with him, declaring that calling God "Father" without truly being a child of God and leading a purer life is not only presumptuous, but also blasphemous — and he even says that when a person who is not truly a child of God offers this prayer, this is actually an invocation of the devil![9]

Furthermore, addressing God as "Father" has important implications not only for our relationship with God but also for our mutual relationships. If we are actually children of the same Father, we are all sisters and brothers. Among many other texts that could be quoted, Augustine's words express it most succinctly:

> Without any distinction among ourselves, we all say, "Our Father." Such goodness! The emperor says it and so does the beggar; the slave says that and so does his master. All say jointly: "Our Father, who art in heaven." By this they declare that they are siblings, for they have a common father. Therefore, let not a master scorn having his slave as a brother — a slave whom the Lord Christ has taken as his brother.[10]

A Bountiful Father

When we speak of God as "Father," we first think of a father providing for his children. The Bible offers abundant support for this emphasis. For instance, in chapter 11 of the Gospel of Luke, which appears almost immediately after Jesus has taught his disciples the prayer we are studying, Jesus says,

> Ask, and it will be given you; search, and you will find; knock, and the door will be opened for you. For everyone who asks receives, and everyone who searches finds, and for everyone who knocks, the door will be opened. Is there anyone among you who, if your child asks for a fish, will give a snake instead of a fish? Or if the child asks for an egg, will give a scorpion? If you then, who are

evil, know how to give good gifts to your children, how much more will the heavenly Father give the Holy Spirit to those who ask him! (Luke 11:9–13)

Another passage that frequently comes to mind is chapter 14 of the Gospel of John: "I will do whatever you ask in my name, so that the Father may be glorified in the Son. If in my name you ask me for anything, I will do it" (John 14:13–14).

Ancient Christian writers certainly believed these words. They insisted on the need for prayer and for trusting that God would answer. But they also insisted that the basic measure of every prayer we offer is the one that the Lord taught. Any petition that opposes what we say in the Lord's Prayer is inappropriate and will not be answered. This is what the words "in my name" mean in John 14:14. To ask in the name of Jesus is to ask for what Jesus has taught us to request. To ask for our own convenience or out of our own self-interest, and certainly to ask in a spirit of anger or competition with others, is not to ask in the name of Jesus, and therefore it is not a prayer that will be answered. For this reason the Lord's Prayer was so important in the devotions of the ancient church and has continued to be so throughout the ages. Our God is not a parent spoiling children by giving them all that they ask. Our God, like a good parent with small children, certainly gives us what we ask for but only when it is for our own good and the good of all creation. This is quite clear in Luke 11 where Jesus promises "good gifts" to those who ask. This truly loving parent will not give us a snake when we ask for fish, nor will God give us a scorpion when we ask for an egg. But because of the same love, if we ask the Father for a scorpion or a snake — something that is not good for us — it will not be given to us. Part of the function of the Lord's Prayer is to help us to see and understand what the heavenly Father is ready to give us by virtue of divine love, and therefore what we ought to ask for.

This relationship between the Lord's Prayer and what we are to ask for becomes even clearer at the end of the passage in Luke, where Jesus promises his disciples the gift of the Holy Spirit. It is precisely this Spirit who shows us how we are to live and teaches us what we are to ask for. Jesus does promise that the heavenly Father will give what we ask for, as long as it is in his name. This is far more than merely repeating the simple formula "in the name of Jesus, Amen." It requires that what we ask for be in agreement with the teachings and purposes of Jesus.

A Trinitarian Prayer

Jesus promises to give us the gift of the Holy Spirit if we ask for it. Paul may have had this prayer in mind when he wrote that the Holy Spirit is "a spirit of adoption. When we cry, 'Abba! Father!' it is that very Spirit bearing witness with our spirit that we are children of God, and if children, then heirs, heirs of God and joint heirs with Christ" (Rom. 8:15–17).

This completes the circle: We can call God "Father" because, by virtue of the Holy Spirit, we have been made "fellow heirs with Christ," who has taken it upon himself to come to be among us, to make us sisters and brothers, and to teach us this prayer by which we dare call God "our Father." It is by the Spirit that we are able to call Jesus "Lord" (Col. 12:3). It is because the Holy Spirit has joined us to Jesus, making us part of his body, that we can call God "Father." Thus, in the Lord's Prayer we address the Father with words taught by the Son and made ours by the Holy Spirit!

The Matter of Gender

It is important, though, to acknowledge that the metaphor of God as "Father" has its limitations, one of which is the authoritarian attitude that earthly parents may adopt, justifying it by claiming that God is Father. Nothing is further from the truth, for this is a misguided use of the metaphor of God as Father. There are always dangers in the metaphors we employ in our faith and devotion. For instance, we speak of Christ as "King." This is an important image, for it points to the power of our Lord and the promise of his final victory. But if we take it in the sense that earthly kings are more like Christ than devout peasants or in the sense that an absolutist regime is better than a democratic one providing greater freedom, we are wrong. Likewise, the image of God as Father is useful in that it points to a God who gives us life, who protects us, and who provides for our needs. It also speaks of a personal God who relates to us as persons. But if we take this image in the sense that God is more like an earthly father than a mother, or in the sense that an earthly father is to have authority over the family in the same way that God has authority over creation, we will again be wrong. Rather than saying that God is like an earthly father, we would do much better to say that earthly fathers should take God as a model of parental love, a love that God is constantly pouring out upon his sons and daughters.

Another important limitation of the image of God as a father must be underscored. Unfortunately, throughout history many believers have thought that referring to God as a father implies that God is exclusively masculine, or that masculinity is closer to God than femininity. That is certainly not the case. God is not only like the warrior defending his people but also like the hen gathering her chicks (Matt. 27:37; Luke 14:13). God is at once both a father and more than any earthly father, both a mother and more than any earthly mother.

Here we encounter a semantic problem. In many modern languages other than English, our father and our mother taken together are called our fathers. In these languages no other expression exists to refer jointly to one's parents. I well remember when I would come back from school with a note in Spanish that had to be signed by "a father or tutor" ("*un padre o tutor*"), which my mother had just as much authority to sign as did my father. (This use of the masculine form to refer to both genders is clearly a reflection of a culture that has long been shaped by male dominance.) Similarly, when the Greek New Testament uses a masculine plural noun, its meaning may also include women. This means, for instance, that when Paul addresses the readers of one of his epistles as "brothers," we are fully justified in translating this either as "brothers" or as "brothers and sisters." It also means that references to God as "Father" may also be understood as references to God as "Parent." Unfortunately, in English the word *parent* is rather impersonal and does not usually emphasize the love and care of a mother or a father.

Throughout history, people have made serious attempts to make it clear that God isn't masculine, and that femininity is just as close to God as is masculinity. One of the most interesting examples is the anchorite, or religious recluse, Julian of Norwich, who, while normally speaking of Jesus in masculine terms, would also refer to "Jesus, our mother." In the Old Testament, particularly in Proverbs 8, the Wisdom that dwells in God is spoken of in feminine terms, described as a woman who says that from the beginning, before all of creation, she was with God. John followed this model in the prologue to his Gospel, where what he says about the Word of God is based on what Proverbs says about Wisdom. Soon, since Jesus is the Wisdom of God, it became common to call him Holy Wisdom or "Saint Sophia." (The famous cathedral of Constantinople, called Saint Sophia, was not dedicated to a saint by that name but to Jesus himself as the eternal Wisdom or *Sophia* of God.)

All this should make it clear that when we address God as our Father in the Lord's Prayer, we are simply using a traditional expression, and we certainly are not saying anything that couldn't be expressed by also calling God "Mother" or "loving Parent."

God Is Love

We need to explore one more important dimension of calling God "Father" or "Mother," which is one more thing the Lord's Prayer teaches us regarding our relationship with God. We frequently quote the words in the First Epistle of John, "God is love" (4:8). When we quote these words, we usually mean that God, as a father or mother, creates us, protects us, and provides us with what we need. But there's another element in the love of a parent that we often forget, but it is actually one of the most important and costly dimensions of parental love. When a responsible couple decides to have children, they know that they will be giving life to beings that are separate individuals. The children may be similar to the parents, but they will have their own personalities, make their own decisions, and choose their own paths. Those deciding to bring them to life know that their children will not always obey them. Quite possibly someday those very children will cause them great pain. But despite all this, the parents decide to have a child. Furthermore, no matter how much parents bemoan the bad decisions and the waywardness of their children, it would be much more painful if their offspring were incapable of making their own decisions, of being "another" that is not the parents. The love for a being who does not even exist yet is so great that, even knowing of that otherness with its potential for rebellion and disobedience, a couple decides to have and to love such a child.

Something similar is meant by the affirmation that this God to whom we pray as Father is love. This love is not limited to giving us life, sustenance, and protection, but it also includes creating beings who will be "others" before God. Creation is not God; it is another. This God of ours who is love has decided to create other realities in addition to Godself. This other reality is a sign of a love so amazing that we have been given the power to follow God's directions as

45

well as to reject them. Furthermore, at one time or another we all rebel against this creator God to whose love we refer when we pray "Our Father."

This too was known by ancient Christians. Among them was St. Augustine, one of the greatest theologians of all time. In his dialogue *On Free Will*, Augustine places a question on the lips of his companion Evodius: "Why has God given humans free will if without it they would have been unable to sin?"[11] Augustine opens his answer by declaring that this free will that humans have received has been given to them precisely so that they may be able to live righteously and thus to attain communion with God:

> If humans are a good creation of God and they can only act righteously when they so decide, it follows that they must have freedom of the will, without which they would never be able to act righteously. Even though free will is the origin of sin, this does not mean that God has given it to us so that we will sin. There is, therefore, a sufficient reason for God having given us this free will, and it is that without it humans could never live righteously.[12]

In other words, God's love for humans is similar to — although far above — that of a mother or father for her or his children. This similarity includes the desire to see them grow freely and fully in spite of the danger — and perhaps even the certainty — that they will somehow be disobedient.

It's all this, and much more, that we affirm when we address God as Father in prayer. Our purpose here isn't simply to learn more about the Lord's Prayer but rather to live it more fully. Therefore, before turning to another chapter, let us return once more to this prayer that the Lord taught us and that should be ours at every moment:

Our Father who art in heaven, hallowed be thy name. Thy kingdom come. Thy will be done on earth as it is in heaven. Give us this day our daily bread. And forgive us our debts, as we forgive our debtors. Lead us not into temptation. But deliver us from evil. For thine is the kingdom, and the power, and the glory forever. Amen.

3

Our Father **Who Art in Heaven**, hallowed
be thy name. Thy kingdom come. Thy will
be done on earth as it is in heaven. Give us
this day our daily bread. And forgive us our
debts, as we forgive our debtors. Lead us not
into temptation. But deliver us from evil.
For thine is the kingdom, and the power,
and the glory forever. Amen.

Where Is God?

We now come to a clause in the Lord's Prayer that many ancient interpreters found difficult and that even today leads some people to think the entire prayer is outmoded. For example, several decades ago a Russian cosmonaut, upon returning from space, declared that he had traveled through the sky seeking God everywhere and had never seen him. This observation was both childish, because it was something that a five-year-old would have said, and political, because the cosmonaut was simply echoing the views of the officially atheistic regime that then ruled the Soviet Union.

While that cosmonaut's words were ridiculous, we must confess that it's difficult to understand what we mean when we say that God is "in heaven." We know that God isn't confined to any particular place. God is omnipresent and is never absent — although sometimes the divine presence is hidden from us. Certainly, this can't mean that God is only in heaven and not where we now are. Then why do we address God as "Our Father, who art in heaven"?

Interestingly, Tertullian, commenting in the late second or early third century on the Lord's Prayer, simply ignored this difficult phrase, moving from "Our Father" to "hallowed be thy name." In

TEACH US TO PRAY

the third century, Cyprian, the Bishop of Carthage, who called Tertullian "the teacher," followed the same procedure.

Also in the third century, the well-known Alexandrian philosopher and theologian Origen clearly expressed the difficulty when he wrote,

> When we hear that the Father of the saints is in heaven, we are not to imagine that he is circumscribed to a material form, and that it is as such that he dwells in heaven. This would make God lesser than the heavens, for they would contain him, and that which contains is always greater than what is contained. But the ineffable vastness of God's divinity requires that we affirm that all things are in him and that he sustains all of them.[1]

In brief, Origen means that God can't be in a particular place as a piece of furniture is in the living room or as a star is in heaven — or, as Luther would say, as a dove is in its cote. What do we mean then when we say that our Father is "in heaven"? Origen answers the question in the same way he deals with other passages that are difficult to interpret: he reads Scripture as a vast allegory — or, as he would say, by means of a spiritual reading. To bolster this interpretation, Origen reminds us that according to Genesis God was "walking in the garden" (Gen. 3:8). Origen points out that this can't mean that God was literally walking along a garden path but rather that God was present to the humans in the garden. In the same way, Origen claims that the clause "who art in heaven" should be interpreted in the sense that "it is thus that God is in heaven, meaning in every saint bearing the image of the heavenly or of Christ, through which all who are being saved are like the lights and stars in heaven."[2] Thus, according to Origen, when we say that God is "in heaven," what we really mean is that God is in us.

Eventually most ancient theologians followed Origen's path in this regard. Thus, for instance, St. Augustine seems to agree with Origen when he declares,

> *Our Father, who art in heaven* means "who art in the saints and the righteous." In truth, God is not encompassed by any place. The heavens are certainly the most excellent part of the world; but even so they are still material, and they cannot exist except in space. If one were to imagine that God is up in the heavens, meaning by that the higher regions of the universe, one could also claim that birds are better than humans, because they live closer to God.[3]

However, even though this may be true to an extent, we all know that, no matter how faithful or how dedicated we are to the service of the Lord, we can't really claim that when we pray and say that God is in heaven we mean that God is within us!

Heaven

Therefore, we must consider what we really mean when we pray to God "who art in heaven." It may help to remember that the word *heaven* has traditionally had two different meanings, both appropriate and valuable. First, when we use the word *heaven* — and certainly when it was used in antiquity — we mean that vast space above us that we also call "the sky." In this sense, heaven or "the heavens" includes the blue atmosphere above us, as well as the most distant galaxies. When we look at the sky or the heavens in this sense, we see something of the overwhelming glory of God. This is why the psalmist declares, "The heavens are telling the glory of God; and the firmament proclaims his handiwork" (Ps. 19:1). And in another psalm we read, "When I look at your heavens, the work of your fingers, the moon and the stars that you have established; what are human beings that you are mindful of them?" (Ps. 8:3–4). When we say that we see God "in the heavens," meaning in the sky, we aren't declaring that God is "up there" but rather that when we look at the sky we can sense God's presence. Likewise, we can say that God is in Scripture or in a mother's love. But this doesn't mean that somehow God is contained in Scripture or in that mother's love. Instead, we mean that God is active in these things and we can sense God.

However, when Scripture says that God is in a particular place, this means much more than what Origen would have us believe. Although we cannot limit God to one particular place, it is clear throughout the Old Testament that God is present in the temple in a particular way. The people of Israel knew that God had been with them in their exile in Babylon, and therefore God wasn't limited to Jerusalem or to the temple. But even so, the temple was the specific place where God's presence was made known to the people and where they worshiped God, as it says in the oft-quoted psalm, "The Lord is in his holy temple" (Ps. 11:4). In the New Testament, where again God is clearly present everywhere and in every moment, we also find the notion of a particular presence of God in Christ, so that Paul can say that God was in Christ "reconciling the world to himself" (2 Cor. 5:19). Therefore, affirming that God is "in heaven" doesn't mean that we are limiting God to a particular place as if it were not possible for God to be elsewhere at the same time.

This paradox of God being omnipresent and yet being particularly present in certain places and circumstances was clearly expressed by King Solomon when, on the occasion of the dedication of the First Temple, he said,

> But will God indeed dwell on the earth? Even heaven and the highest heaven cannot contain you, much less this house that I have built! Regard your servant's prayer and his plea, O Lord my God, heeding the cry and the prayer that your servant prays to you today; that your eyes may be open night and day toward

this house, the place of which you said, 'My name shall be there,' that you may heed the prayer that your servant prays toward this place. Hear the plea of your servant and of your people Israel when they pray toward this place; O hear in heaven your dwelling place; heed and forgive. (1 Kings 8:27–30)

Returning to the clause "who art in heaven" and to its interpretation, we must also take a second meaning of *heaven* into account, for in Israel as well as in the early church the words *heaven* and *heavens* were often used in reference to Godself. For the Hebrews, the name of God was so sacred it could never be pronounced. Instead, people would sometimes refer to God as "the heavens" or "the throne." This seems to have carried on into some Christian circles. Note that what Luke in his Gospel calls "the kingdom of God" Matthew generally calls "the kingdom of heaven," apparently meaning the kingdom of one so exalted that one should avoid speaking his name.

If we interpret the words "who art in heaven" in this sense, then they are actually a radical affirmation of divine immensity. God is such that one can say only that God is in Godself. God's presence can certainly be seen in all of creation and particularly in Jesus Christ. But the only one able to contain God is Godself — which reminds us of the words that God speaks to Moses saying, "I am who I am" (Exod. 13:14). God's being and God's presence can be defined only in terms of God. Note that this is also close to what we mean when we say that the angels or the faithful "are in heaven." By this we don't mean that they are in some particular place high above us, but rather that they are in the very presence of God.

Heaven and Earth

Frequently in the Bible, as well as in the ancient creeds of the church, heaven and earth are mentioned jointly. This is true in the very first verse of Genesis, where we read that God created "the heavens and the earth." At the other end of Scripture, in chapter 21 of the book of Revelation, John declares that he saw "a new heaven and a new earth" (Rev. 21:1).

When these two words, *heaven* and *earth*, are used jointly, they usually mean all that exists. It's not simply a matter of dividing all that exists in two categories or two sorts of things, one called "heaven" and the other "earth" — the latter meaning all that exists around us and the former all that is above. It's rather a way of declaring that there is nothing that God didn't make. This is what the Apostles' Creed means when it declares that God is "maker of heaven and earth." And it's also what the Nicene Creed means by affirming that God is maker of "all things visible and invisible." When employed jointly, the two words, *heaven* and *earth*, refer to all reality, that which we see and that which we don't see, that which we understand and that which we don't understand.

If we look once again at Solomon's prayer at the dedication of the temple, quoted above, we note that Solomon begins by declaring that "heaven and the highest heaven cannot contain you," but later he asks God to "hear in heaven your dwelling place." Clearly, the same word "heaven" has two different meanings here. In the first case it could easily be translated as "sky." But in the second it's much more than that. There it refers to the mystery in which God dwells. All of the earth and even the sky cannot contain God. But one can say that God dwells in heaven, meaning that God is surrounded by mystery.

Karl Barth, arguably the most important theologian of the twentieth century, expressed this by saying,

> We may and indeed we must say, that in the two concepts of heaven and earth, single and in their conjunction, we are confronted with what we might call the Christian doctrine of the crea-

ture. But these two concepts do not signify a kind of equivalent to what we usually call today a picture of the world, even though it can be said that some of the old picture of the world is reflected in them. . . . Heaven is the creation inconceivable to man; earth is the creation conceivable to him. I concur, therefore, in the explanation of heaven and earth, given in the Nicene Creed, as *visibilia et invisibilia*. . . . When Holy Scripture, with whose usage we here link up, speaks of heaven, we are not to understand by that simply what we usually term heaven, the atmospheric or even stratospheric heaven, but a creaturely reality, which is utterly superior to this "heaven."[4]

This is the second meaning of the word *heaven*. In this sense, the heavens are all that we cannot know, not simply in the sense that we don't understand it yet, as is the case, for instance, with a law of physics, but rather because the very nature of heaven is a mystery beyond our capabilities. As Barth says, in contrast to earth, which is the sum of all that we can understand and explore be it on the planet where we live or in the most distant space, heaven is mystery beyond our understanding, beyond our expressions, and even beyond our imagination. Looking back at the comments of that Soviet cosmonaut mentioned at the beginning of this chapter, we may say that what he saw, even though it certainly was part of the sky, in truth was just another part of what we properly call *earth* — that is, what our minds can understand or at least explore. *Earth* is all that exists within time and space. When thus defined, it's clear that the cosmonaut, no matter how far he had traveled, was still within the sphere of earth.

This idea was already expressed a few years before the adventures of that cosmonaut, and with a good measure of irony, by one of my professors at Yale Divinity School. We had awakened that morning to the news that the Soviets had managed to launch Sputnik, the first human-made satellite, into space, and newscasters were reporting that humankind had finally begun the conquest of space. Before beginning his lecture that morning, Prof. H. Richard Niebuhr said, "Once upon a time there was in the middle of the Pacific Ocean a large ship battered by the waves and loaded with tons of potatoes. One good day, a worm within one of the potatoes was able to chew through the potato's skin and with great enthusiasm returned to the center of the potato saying, 'We have conquered space!'" In other words, the apparently amazing news that had become headlines in our day was no more than taking a peek at the suburbs of a small planet within a solar system that is no more than part of a vast galaxy amidst a countless multitude of much larger galaxies. All that Sputnik had done was to visit a new place within this immense part of creation that could still be called earth. We weren't even beginning to move into the outskirts of the mystery that we call the heavens.

We know that both time and space are parts of this earth that we can explore and partly understand, and yet they place us face to face with the inscrutable mystery of heaven. We can't conceive of space as being endless; but it's equally impossible for us to think that it ends, with no further space beyond. The same may be said about time, for while it's impossible for us to think of time as having no beginning or end, it's equally impossible for us to think that it may have a beginning or an end. Therefore, the earth itself, this wide scope of what is reasonable and comprehensible, forces us to think of heaven, that which we can only suspect and perhaps begin to glimpse through faith.

If we take this into account, praying to our Father "who art in heaven" affirms that this one whom we dare call Father by God's grace and mercy is not only the God whose revelation comes to us on earth and in history but is also the ineffable one who is far beyond any human description or understanding — existing in that heaven that our minds can't even conceive. This God whom we worship, even while being our Father, is also the God of the heavens, the inescapable one, the profound mystery that we are too small to even begin to conceive. And yet, this one loves us as a Father!

John Calvin expressed this while commenting on the clause of the Lord's Prayer that we are discussing:

> That he is in heaven is added. From this we are not immediately to reason that he is bound, shut up, and surrounded, by the circumference of heaven, as by a barred enclosure. For Solomon confesses that the heaven of heavens cannot contain him. And he himself says through the prophet that heaven is his seat, and the earth, his footstool. By this he obviously means that he is not confined to any particular region but is diffused through all things. But our minds, so crass are they, could not have conceived his unspeakable glory otherwise. Consequently, it has been signified to us by "heaven," for we can behold nothing more sublime or majestic than this. While, therefore, wherever our senses comprehend anything they commonly attach it to that place, God is set beyond all place, so that when we would seek him we must rise above the perception of body and soul. Secondly, by this expression he is lifted above all chance of either corruption or change. Finally, it signifies that he embraces and holds together the entire universe and controls it by his might. Therefore, it is as if he had been said to be of infinite greatness and loftiness, of incomprehensible essence, of boundless might, and of everlasting immortality. But while we hear this, our thought must be raised higher when God is spoken of, lest we dream up anything earthly or physical about him, lest we measure him by our small measure, or conform his will to our emotions. At the same time our confidence in him must be aroused, since we understand that heaven and earth are ruled by his providence and power.[5]

Our Heavenly Father

Led by the example of the model prayer that the Lord has taught us, we often refer to God as "our heavenly Father." What we've seen in this chapter underscores the enormity of what we're saying. We are claiming that this being whom we call Father not only loves us as a parent and even more than a parent but is also Lord and Creator of all there is. God, this one whom we call *our* Father, is also the inescapable Lord of all. Our heavenly Father is not only right here with us but also beyond the furthest reaches of our mind, our feelings, and even our imagination. We call this one Father because we know that God loves us as children. Yet at the very moment we address God in this way, we come face to face with the ineffable mystery far beyond all that exists. And — what is the most surprising and overwhelming of all — this sovereign Lord of the universe and even beyond the universe is also our Father! Compared with the ineffable majesty of this God whose mystery is inscrutable, we are less than worms. But by the grace of that very mystery, we are God's sons and daughters!

Thus, overwhelmed by the inscrutable greatness of God on the one hand and surprised by unexpected grace on the other, we dare say and also rejoice in saying,

> **Our Father who art in heaven**, hallowed be thy name. Thy kingdom come. Thy will be done on earth as it is in heaven. Give us this day our daily bread. And forgive us our debts, as we forgive our debtors. Lead us not into temptation. But deliver us from evil. For thine is the kingdom, and the power, and the glory forever. Amen.

4

Our Father who art in heaven, **Hallowed Be Thy Name**. Thy kingdom come. Thy will be done on earth as it is in heaven. Give us this day our daily bread. And forgive us our debts, as we forgive our debtors. Lead us not into temptation. But deliver us from evil. For thine is the kingdom, and the power, and the glory forever. Amen.

The Petitions in the Lord's Prayer

We now come to the first petition in the Lord's Prayer. The words we have studied in the last three chapters are not really petitions, but rather an invocation to the one to whom the prayer is directed: "Our Father, who art in heaven." Now we come to the first of seven petitions. The first three are expressions of the nature, will, and promises of God — promises that also place a demand on those who pray for them: (1) *Hallowed be thy name*; (2) *Thy kingdom come*; (3) *Thy will be done on earth as it is in heaven*. The other four are petitions in the strict sense, for in them we ask God to act in our favor: (1) *Give us this day our daily bread*; (2) *And forgive us our debts, as we forgive our debtors*; (3) *Lead us not into temptation*; (4) *But deliver us from evil*. Referring to the first three of these clauses, and then to the other four, Thomas Aquinas said, "These [first three] petitions will therefore come to fruition in the future life, while the other four deal with the needs of the present life."[1] Martin Luther seems to concur, declaring that "the first, second, and third petitions deal with the highest benefits that we receive from Him. . . . In the other four petitions we meet the needs of our daily life and of this poor, weak, temporal existence."[2] In other

words, the first three simply call for the fulfillment of God's promises and therefore are not petitions in the strict sense but rather
are affirmations of the purposes and the nature of God that should
guide the life and faith of believers. Nothing of what we say in
these first three petitions is really up to us, nor is any of it contin-
gent on what we do. What we declare in them is simply a reality
and a promise to which we are to adjust. Let's now turn to the first
petition in the Lord's Prayer.

Can the Perfectly Holy Be Hallowed?

Throughout history Christians have agreed that, when we pray
these words, we aren't really claiming that somehow we can add
holiness to the name of God, but rather we affirm that our lives are
to be modeled after divine holiness. As Scripture says, "Be holy, for I
am holy" (Lev. 11:24; 1 Pet. 1:15–16; see also Matt. 5:48). We see this
already in one of the earliest writings to discuss the Lord's Prayer,
Tertullian's already-quoted *On Prayer*. He affirms that

> . . . when we say, "Hallowed be Thy name," we pray this; that it
> may be hallowed *in us* who are in Him, as well in all others for
> whom the grace of God is still waiting; that we may obey this pre-
> cept, too, in "praying for all," even for our personal enemies. And
> therefore with suspended utterance, not saying, "Hallowed be it
> *in us*, "we say, – "*in all.*"[3]

Half a century later, Cyprian wrote similarly, only now pointing out
that human activity can never make God holier and that therefore
what we really ask for is that our lives may reflect God's holiness:

> After this we say, "Hallowed be Thy name"; not that we wish for
> God that He may be hallowed by our prayers, but that we beseech

of Him that His name may be hallowed in us. But by whom is God sanctified, since He Himself sanctifies? Well, because He says, "Be ye holy, even as I am holy," we ask and entreat, that we who were sanctified in baptism may continue in that which we have begun to be. And this we daily pray for; for we have need of daily sanctification, that we who daily fall away may wash out our sins by continual sanctification.[4]

A few decades after Cyprian, Origen offered the same explanation in a long passage that includes the following words:

> Both in Matthew and in Luke we are told that we are to pray "Hallowed be thy name," as if the name of God were not already holy. This may well lead us to ask how such a thing is possible. . . . Therefore, one who prays must keep this in mind when calling for the hallowing of God's name. It is to this that the Psalmist refers when he says "let us with one mind exalt his name." Thus the Father commands that joining in a single spirit and a single mind we may truly speak of the nature of God. We truly exalt the name of God, for we have shared in the divine presence and have been received by God. Therefore we praise this divine holiness of which God has allowed us to partake.[5]

In other words, when we ask that God's name be hallowed we are in no way suggesting that God could be holier, but we are simply asking God to allow us to partake of divine holiness. On this point all ancient writers agree. As is so often the case, St. Augustine provides us with a clear summary of this point:

> We can now look at what is to be asked for. Since we have already said of whom we are asking and where he dwells, we now move to the first petition. This is *Hallowed be thy name*. We do not ask for

this as if God's name were not holy, but rather that all may praise God as holy; that God be known by all in such a way that nothing will appear holier to them and no one will they fear of offending as much as God.[6]

Except for Origen, all the authors cited so far in this chapter wrote in Latin, but the same interpretation of this petition is found among those who wrote in Greek. Two examples should suffice, Gregory of Nyssa and John Chrysostom. Gregory says,

> When in prayer I say "hallowed be thy name"; but what I seek is that these words may impact me. I ask that through your divine help you will make me pure, righteous, faithful, and that I may abstain from all evil, speak truth, and practice justice. I ask to walk along the straight path, illumined by temperance, adorned by incorruption, beautified by God's virtue and wisdom. I ask that I may be able to look upon things on high and leave aside the earthly, so that my life may be similar to the angels. These and many other similar wishes are included in the brief words, "Hallowed be thy name." The only way in which God's name can be glorified is by means of a virtuous life witnessing to the power of God as the source of our own goodness.[7]

Chrysostom, after commenting on the first words of the Lord's Prayer, adds,

> When therefore He hath reminded us of this nobility [of God], and of the gift from above, and of our equality with our brethren, and of charity; and when He hath removed us from earth, and fixed us in Heaven; let us see what He commands us to ask after this. Not but, in the first place, even that saying alone is sufficient to implant instruction in all virtue. For he who hath called God

Father, and a common Father, would be justly bound to show forth such a conversation, as not to appear unworthy of this nobility, and to exhibit a diligence proportionate to the gift. Yet is He not satisfied with this, but adds, also another clause, thus saying, "Hallowed be Thy name."

Worthy of him who calls God Father, is the prayer to ask nothing before the glory of His Father, but to account all things secondary to the work of praising Him. For "hallowed" is *glorified*. For His own glory He hath complete, and ever continuing the same, but He commands him who prays to seek that He may be glorified also by our life. Which very thing He had said before likewise, "Let your light so shine before men, that they may see your good works, and glorify your Father which is in heaven." Yea, and the seraphim too, giving glory, said on this wise, "Holy, holy, holy." So that "hallowed" means this, *viz.* "glorified." That is, "vouchsafe," saith he, "that we may live so purely, that through us all may glorify Thee." Which thing again appertains unto perfect self-control, to present to all a life so irreprehensible, that every one of the beholders may offer to the Lord the praise due to Him for this.[8]

What Is Sanctification?

While these authors, and many others, agree that when we say "Hallowed be thy name" this doesn't mean that we make God holier, but rather that we ask to reflect divine holiness, we must stop to consider the meaning of holiness or sanctification.

Strictly speaking, holiness belongs only to God. There's no other truly and completely holy being. When properly understood, holiness leads us to admiration, awe, and even terror. Sometimes we forget this, imagining that God's holiness is simply divine purity and goodness and that our own path to holiness is simply to purify our lives progressively. But in Scripture, holiness signifies the unequaled and fearsome character of God. Just one among many examples is the covenant of God with the people on Mount Sinai:

> When Moses had told the words of the people to the LORD, the LORD said to Moses: "Go to the people and consecrate them today and tomorrow. Have them wash their clothes and prepare for the third day, because on the third day the LORD will come down upon Mount Sinai in the sight of all the people. You shall set limits for the people all around, saying, 'Be careful not to go up the mountain or to touch the edge of it. Any who touch the mountain shall be put to death.'" (Exod. 19:9–12)

There are many other similar passages. God's holiness is such that it's impossible to gaze on the divine face and still live (Exod. 33:20). Furthermore, this fearsome divine holiness also touches all that has been set aside for God's service. Thus, anyone who touches the ark of the covenant will die, and those who profane the temple will suffer grievous consequences.

To hallow or to make holy means to set aside for divine service. Thus, as early as the second chapter of Genesis, we read that God "blessed the seventh day and hallowed it" (Gen. 2:3). Making the seventh day holy does not mean that it's especially pure but rather that it is a particular day that God has set aside for purposes established by Godself. In later passages, Scripture mentions the hallowing or sanctification of the people, the sanctification of the temple and its utensils, the sanctification of sacrifices, and so forth. This in turn implies that true sanctification, being set aside for the service of God, has overwhelming dimensions. Biblical holiness does not consist in being morally pure or ritually clean but rather in being set aside for the service of God. It is when this setting aside takes place and hallowed places and people point to God's holiness that the name of God is hallowed among God's people.

Sanctification, Profanation, and Religion

Even though the name of God cannot be made holier by human action, the Bible does speak repeatedly about the profanation of that name and blasphemy against it. Such blasphemy or profanation isn't limited to religious matters but has various dimensions. In the laws of the Pentateuch we read repeatedly about the need not to profane the name of God. In some cases, that profanation involves praying to other gods and the resulting punishment. For instance, Leviticus 20:1–5 commands that any offering their offspring to Molech are to be stoned to death, for in that sacrifice to Molech they are "defiling my sanctuary and profaning my holy name."

We see something similar in Ezekiel 20:39, where God declares that not only idols themselves but also offerings presented to God while one actually worships idols are an abomination and an offense against God's holy name: "Go serve your idols, everyone of you now and hereafter, if you will not listen to me; but my holy name you shall no more profane with your gifts and your idols."

In other cases the profanation is in taking what actually belongs to God or in offering to God a false sort of worship. Thus, in Leviticus 22:2, God commands Aaron and his sons "to deal carefully with the sacred donations of the people of Israel, which they dedicate to me, so that they may not profane my holy name."

Sanctification and Profanation beyond Religious Matters

Although the name of God is profaned by following other gods or blaspheming against God, profanation also takes place when God is disobeyed in other aspects of life. Ezekiel 43:4–10, while affirming the holiness of the temple, also declares that God's holiness can also be profaned beyond the confines of this sacred space by means of unjust or impure actions:

As the glory of the LORD entered the temple by the gate facing east, the spirit lifted me up, and brought me into the inner court; and the glory of the LORD filled the temple.

> While the man was standing beside me, I heard someone speaking to me out of the temple. He said to me: Mortal, this is the place of my throne and the place for the soles of my feet, where I will reside among the people of Israel forever. The house of Israel shall no more defile my holy name, neither they nor their kings, by their whoring, and by the corpses of their kings at their death. When they placed their threshold by my threshold and their doorposts beside my doorposts, with only a wall between me and them, they were defiling my holy name by their abominations that they committed; therefore I have consumed them in my anger. Now let them put away their idolatry and the corpses of their kings far from me, and I will reside among them forever.

> As for you, mortal, describe the temple to the house of Israel, and let them measure the pattern; and let them be ashamed of their iniquities.

In other words, even when the holy house of God itself is not profaned, the attitudes and actions of the people and their lives beyond the confines of the temple can also profane the holy name of God. And when this is done in the proximity of the temple the profanation is even more serious.

Sanctification, Purification, and Justice

The abominations of the people and its leaders beyond the confines of the temple aren't only religious in nature. They include issues of justice and equity. This profanation, according to Jeremiah 34:15–16, consists in returning to unjust practices that should have been left behind:

You yourselves recently repented and did what was right in my sight by proclaiming liberty to one another, and you made a covenant before me in the house that is called by my name; but then you turned around and profaned my name when each of you took back your male and female slaves, whom you had set free according to their desire, and you brought them again into subjection to be your slaves.

This is also made clear in a passage from Proverbs and another from James. The first of these is particularly pertinent to our subject for, as we will see in another chapter, it lays the foundation for another petition in the Lord's Prayer:

> Two things I ask of you;
>> do not deny them to me before I die:
> Remove far from me falsehood and lying;
>> give me neither poverty nor riches;
>> feed me with the food that I need,
> or I shall be full, and deny you,
>> and say, "Who is the Lord?"
> or I shall be poor, and steal,
>> and profane the name of my God. (Prov. 30:7–9)

The person who prays in this way fears that need may lead to theft. However, the basis of this fear isn't the possibility of discovery or punishment but rather fear that such conduct will profane the name of God. The people of God are to be holy because God is holy, and therefore conditions leading to theft are an abomination not only against the laws of society but also against God, whose holiness is profaned in the very act of profaning the holiness of the people.

The following passage from James affirms that the rich who oppress the poor and make use of the courts and their laws to justify

such oppression are profaning the name of God. This is partly because the name of God doesn't cover just the rich and powerful but
also, particularly, the poor and weak. Therefore, oppressing and
exploiting the poor is a profanation of the holy name of God. James
says it quite starkly:

> Listen, my beloved brothers and sisters. Has not God chosen the
> poor in the world to be rich in faith and to be heirs of the king-
> dom that he has promised to those who love him? But you have
> dishonored the poor. Is it not the rich who oppress you? Is it not
> they who drag you into court? Is it not they who blaspheme the
> excellent name that was invoked over you? (James 2:5–7)

Blasphemy and Community

The biblical laws against blasphemy are designed to safeguard the
holiness, not only of the individual, but also and above all of the
entire people of God. What is the difference between blasphemy
and disbelief? One who doesn't believe in a particular god may deny
and disobey that god, but strictly speaking this is not blasphemy.
Blasphemy is an evil that can take place only within the community
of faith — which makes it more damnable. Israel didn't expect the
Ninevites or the Babylonians to believe in the God of Israel. Since
such people didn't know the true God, they were unbelieving gentiles but not blasphemers. We often forget that, both in Israel and
in Christianity, faith is a matter of community. Those who don't
belong to the community and therefore don't ask that the name of
God be hallowed do not blaspheme by disobeying God and following their own paths.

At various points in its history, the church has applied laws
against blasphemy to people who actually did not belong to the
church and thereby has turned these laws into laws of oppression

against nonbelievers. Although today fewer Christians follow this path, many still do. Something similar happens when, in some of the most radically Muslim countries, Christians are accused of blasphemy and condemned simply because they do not accept the official religion of the land.

Sanctification and Witness

The many passages quoted at the beginning of this chapter point out that when we ask that God's name be hallowed, we are not expecting that God's holy name will be made holier, but rather we are asking that the divine holiness may be shown in us. Therefore, when we say, "Hallowed be thy name," we are asking God to make us holy in such a way that our lives will be a witness to the divine holiness. As Ezekiel says when he bemoans the behavior of Israel among the nations, "But when they came to the nations, wherever they came, they profaned my holy name, in that it was said of them, 'These are the people of the LORD, and yet they had to go out of his land.' But I had concern for my holy name, which the house of Israel had profaned among the nations to which they came" (Ezek. 36:20–21). And in Romans 2:23–24 the apostle Paul echoes the same complaint, saying, "You that boast in the law, do you dishonor God by breaking the law? For, as it is written, 'The name of God is blasphemed among the Gentiles because of you.'"

Sanctification, Consecration, and Purity

Up to this point in the discussion of holiness, little has been said about purity and morality. There is no doubt that Scripture declares categorically that moral corruption profanes the name of God. But it doesn't say, as many imagine, that rejecting such corruption makes one holy. In other words, moral purity does not make one a saint; rather, it is holiness that leads to moral purity and requires it. In the Old Testament, the people of God are holy, not because they always obey God, but rather because God has set them apart for God's service. The same is true in the New Testament regarding the church. The church is holy not because it is morally pure nor because its members are devout. The church is holy because it is a body whose Head, Jesus Christ, is holy. Believers are holy not because they are pure but because they are part of this holy body of the Holy One. Purity does not make us holy; rather, holiness calls us to purity.

This is why the Bible frequently refers to believers in Christ as saints. Surprising as this may be, their being called saints doesn't necessarily mean that they are pure and obedient. Note that Paul addresses his First Epistle to the Corinthians "to those who are sanctified in Christ Jesus, called to be saints" (1 Cor. 1:2). Then he says, "It is actually reported that there is sexual immorality among you, and of a kind that is not found even among pagans" (1 Cor. 5:1). The Corinthians are saints not because they are pure and obey the commandments of God nor because all the members of their church are pure. On the contrary, it is precisely because they are holy that they are called to be pure and obey the divine commandments; their impurity is blasphemy against the hallowed name of God.

We can see that at the present time, the holiness of believers is not fully manifested but is a promise. Thus, Paul says not only that the Corinthians have been sanctified, but also that they are "called to be saints" — an expression he repeats in Romans 1:7. Since holiness is not ours, but God's, it is not something that we can claim on the basis of our own virtue, but rather it is both the gift and the promise of God, and therefore has both a present and a future dimension. We are already sanctified, and yet we are called to be saints.

The same idea is found in an already-quoted passage from Cyprian, where he says, "We ask and entreat, that we who were sanctified in baptism may continue in that which we have begun to be." As Cyprian sees matters, by being joined to the body of Christ in baptism we have already been made saints. It is this that "we have begun to be." But at the same time we must persevere and move ahead in holiness, and this results in a life of obedience, justice, and purity.

This is of the utmost importance, for here lies the difference between being holy and being "holier than thou." Holiness is a gift of God that calls us to obedience. Being "holier than thou" is the result of seeking to attain holiness by being better and more obedient. The latter case leads to so-called saints who seem to believe that their task is to criticize the failures of others, whereas the truly holy ones acknowledge that any virtue they may have isn't theirs but is rather a gift from the only one who is truly holy.

This has implications not only for individual Christians but also for the church as a whole. Once again, the church is holy not because it is pure but is called to be pure because it is holy. Not recognizing the source of holiness is the motive of many conflicts and divisions within the church. If the holiness of the church depends on the purity of its members, we must confess that there is no such thing as a holy church. We often forget this, and the result is that in any given church some consider themselves holier than the rest and break away in order to create a truly holy church. Frequently, shortly after that division, some people in the supposedly holier church decide that others are not sufficiently holy and break away to form still another church. And so on ad infinitum.

When this happens, holiness is being confused with being purer, stricter, or more committed than others. The error lies in believing that the holiness of the church is the result of the purity and obedience of its members, when true holiness is a gift of the Holy One. Certainly, holiness calls for obedience, and sin then becomes a profanation not only of our own holiness, but also of the name of God, which is to be hallowed.

TEACH US TO PRAY

This leads finally to an issue that Christians have frequently debated in centuries past: are the virtues of pagans real virtues or are they rather vices? Great figures such as Augustine and Calvin have held that the virtues of nonbelievers are of no value for they are not grounded in faith. However, on the basis of the foregoing one may well say that it is indeed possible to be virtuous without being holy — that is, without being grafted into the body of Christ. The virtues of pagans and nonbelievers are true, admirable, and valuable virtues; but such virtues do not make them holy, just as our virtues do not make us holy.

In conclusion, when we pray "Hallowed be thy name" we are asking that we, whose holy Head makes us holy, may reflect God's holiness in our own sanctification, and that this be made manifest in a life and a community that witness to the holy love of God.

On this basis we dare say:

Our Father who art in heaven, hallowed be thy name. Thy kingdom come. Thy will be done on earth as it is in heaven. Give us this day our daily bread. And forgive us our debts, as we forgive our debtors. Lead us not into temptation. But deliver us from evil. For thine is the kingdom, and the power, and the glory forever. Amen.

5

Our Father who art in heaven, hallowed be thy name. **Thy Kingdom Come**. Thy will be done on earth as it is in heaven. Give us this day our daily bread. And forgive us our debts, as we forgive our debtors. Lead us not into temptation. But deliver us from evil. For thine is the kingdom, and the power, and the glory forever. Amen.

The Present and Coming Kingdom

In the last chapter we saw that the holiness of the church and of its members is both a present reality and a future promise. Asking that the name of God be hallowed is asking for what is already a promise. In a way, the same is true when we ask that the reign of God will come, for God is and has always been king. Gregory of Nyssa expressed this in the fourth century when he said, "In the next clause we ask that the kingdom of God may come. Does this mean that the one who is already king of the universe should now become king? If God's perfection is such that it cannot be improved, how can we believe that something that was not before will now come to be?"[1] In the last chapter we saw that in Christ we have been sanctified, but also that in him we will be made holy. Something similar is true of the kingdom of God. On the one hand, Jesus tells his disciples that "the kingdom of God is among you" (Luke 17:21). But on the other, Jesus tells his disciples that they are to pray for the coming of the kingdom. Almost immediately after declaring in chapter 17 of Luke that the kingdom of God is "among you," in the rest of the chapter, Jesus tells his disciples that the kingdom will come when least expected.

In the third century, Cyprian had wrestled with the same question, coming to the conclusion that the kingdom of God is both a present reality and a promise to be fulfilled. He says,

> There follows in the prayer, Thy kingdom come. We ask that the kingdom of God may be set forth to us, even as we also ask that His name may be sanctified in us. For when does God not reign, or when does that begin with Him which both always has been, and never ceases to be? We pray that our kingdom, which has been promised us by God, may come, which was acquired by the blood and passion of Christ; that we who first are His subjects in the world, may hereafter reign with Christ when He reigns, as He Himself promises.[2]

Further study of Luke 17 helps us understand the teachings of Jesus regarding the kingdom of God. First, notice that verses 20 and 21 are addressed to Pharisees who have asked him about the time of the coming of the kingdom. In quoting Jesus's answer, Luke uses a phrase that, at the time, was generally employed in reference to natural phenomena or the events surrounding a particular person: "The kingdom of God is not coming with things that can be observed; nor will they say, 'Look, here it is!' or 'There it is!'" In other words, it is impossible to figure out when the kingdom will come by studying natural phenomena, or historical events, or even prophecies. Jesus repeatedly declared that it is impossible to know the time of his return or of the establishment of the kingdom. At the beginning of the book of Acts, when his disciples ask him whether he is about to restore the kingdom, he tells them in no uncertain terms that this is not their business: "It is not for you to know the times or periods that the Father has set by his own authority" (Acts 1:7).

Notice, too, that the words "the kingdom of God is among you" in Luke 17 aren't addressed to the disciples but rather to the Pharisees who have asked him about the time when the kingdom will be established. At that time, just as today, many speculated about the date when the kingdom of God would come. Here Jesus tells the Pharisees that it is impossible to tell the date or time but also that, in a way, "the kingdom of God is among you." As we have seen in several of the quotations above, it was common in early times — as it still is today — to understand these words of Jesus to mean that believers already have the kingdom of God in their hearts. In the fourth century, Ambrose wrote, "The kingdom of God came when God's grace came to you, for it is Jesus himself who says that 'the kingdom of God is within you.'"[3] This interpretation and others like it suggest that, instead of being translated as "the kingdom of God is among you," Jesus's words should be understood as "the kingdom of God is within you." On this point, looking at the Greek text offers little help, for both translations, "among you," and "within you," are legitimate. But reading the entire passage, we find it difficult to understand how Jesus first tells the Pharisees that the kingdom of God is already within them, and then, in verse 22, turns to his disciples to tell them about the kingdom and its coming.

The best possible interpretation of these verses would be that Jesus is saying to the Pharisees that the kingdom of God is already present among them precisely because Jesus is there. It is as if he were saying, "The kingdom of God is already here, for I am among you." In other words, the very presence of Jesus is the presence of the kingdom. And since Jesus repeatedly told his disciples that he would return, he is referring to his return when he speaks of the future kingdom. One might even say that Jesus is not only the king but also the kingdom itself. Wherever he is, the kingdom is present. For this reason, John the Baptist goes out to prepare the way for Jesus by declaring that "the kingdom of God has come near" (Matt. 3:2).

Taking all this into account, we can conclude that when we pray "thy kingdom come" we are echoing that very ancient Christian prayer, "Come, Lord Jesus!" On this point, Cyprian declares,

> Christ Himself, dearest brethren, however, may be the kingdom of God, whom we day by day desire to come, whose advent we crave to be quickly manifested to us. For since He is Himself the Resurrection, since in Him we rise again, so also the kingdom of God may be understood to be Himself, since in Him we shall reign. But we do well in seeking the kingdom of God, that is, the heavenly kingdom, because there is also an earthly kingdom.[4]

Therefore, believers insist that the kingdom of God, just like the sanctification of the faithful, is both a present reality and a future promise. As Thomas Aquinas has said, this is the second of three petitions that "will be perfectly fulfilled in the future life."[5] Thus, this clause in the Lord's Prayer is both a petition and an expression of confidence in the divine purposes.

The Nature of the Kingdom

Much is said in Scripture regarding the kingdom of God, but this is not the place to explore it in any detail. It is important, though, to take into account what Jesus himself says regarding the nature of the kingdom. In several parables in the Gospel of Matthew, Jesus says that the kingdom of God "may be compared to . . ." or "is like. . . ." In Matthew 13:24–37 we find the parable of the tares, or weeds, growing among the wheat. Here we see that it is best not to pull up the tares, for the wheat will be destroyed along with them. Both must be allowed to grow until the time comes for the harvest, when the wheat will be separated from the weeds. At the end of the same chapter, Jesus tells another parable leading in the same direction, although now instead of using agricultural images he draws his example from the experience of fishing. He reminds his readers that a net thrown into the sea catches all sorts of fish, but when it is drawn ashore the good fish are preserved and the others are cast aside. As with the field of wheat and weeds, the net will include both the just and the unjust until the day of judgment. A similar teaching appears in Matthew 22:2–4, which tells of a king who prepares a great wedding feast. When the original invitees reject his invitation, the king orders his servants to go out and call in all sorts of people. But even then, the king orders that some people who have come in with the rest be cast out. Taken as a whole, these three parables — and others like them — make two basic points regarding the kingdom and its coming. First, it is not up to the servants of God to decide who is good wheat and who is a weed, who are the good fish and who are not, who are truly invited and who are not. That task is reserved for the final day — the harvest, the drawing of the net, the wedding feast. Thus, the kingdom of God moves ahead and calls its subjects even while all sorts of evil may be practiced.

The second point becomes clear as we note that the same chapter of Matthew includes two very brief parables that show what Jesus would say more openly in other circumstances: that the kingdom of God is hidden in what seems small and weak but is much greater than one might imagine and more powerful than it seems. The parable of someone planting a tiny mustard seed and the parallel parable of the woman placing a bit of yeast within a larger measure of flour both illustrate this point. Both the seed and the yeast would seem to be as nothing, and yet they have great power that will later come forth.

Among the parables about the kingdom, several deal with what interpreters call "the great reversal": the first shall be last, the least shall be great, and so forth. One of these is found in Matthew 20:1–16. This is a story about a man who hired workers for his vineyard at various times of the day, so that they did not all work the same number of hours. At the end of the day, he paid a full day's wage to those who had come last. Then he paid the same amount to all, including those who had worked for the whole day. At the end of the parable Jesus comments, "So the last will be first, and the first will be last."

This great reversal is more notable in several of the parables that Luke records. A Samaritan, a person whom Jews despised and considered unclean, shows compassion far beyond that of the religious leaders of Israel — a priest and a Levite. A barren fig tree receives more attention and fertilizer than a fruitful vineyard. The ninety-nine sheep that have faithfully stayed with the shepherd are abandoned in the wilderness while he goes after the one that was lost. Therefore, "there will be more joy in heaven over one sinner who repents than over ninety-nine righteous persons who need no repentance" (Luke 15:7). A woman who mislays one coin out of ten invites her neighbors to celebrate her finding the one that was lost but does not seem to think much about the nine that were never lost. An apparently good and obedient son, who remains with his father while his brother squanders his inheritance, does not join the banquet when his brother returns. A Pharisee — that is, a deeply religious person — goes to pray in the temple, boasting of his purity and obedience to the divine commandments, while a sinful tax collector who does not even dare raise his eyes to heaven is justified sooner than the righteous Pharisee (Luke 18:9–14).

Glimpses of the Kingdom

When we say that we await the kingdom of God, does that mean that we see no signs of it now? Certainly not! It's true that we see no signs telling us when it will come. But we do see signs of the kingdom wherever the love and will of God are revealed. Even though the kingdom is a future expectation, a foretaste of it can also be a present experience. We can experience such signs of the kingdom wherever love is manifest and conquers hatred and evil. We see it when old grievances are forgiven. We see it when barriers separating people from one another are broken. We see it when people fleeing terror or poverty are made welcome. We see it wherever the mission of Jesus is made real, when good news is proclaimed to the poor, when the captives are set free, and when the blind recover sight.

Therefore, those of us who pray "Thy kingdom come" must be willing to tear down barriers, to forgive enemies, to bring good news to the poor, and to liberate the oppressed. When we do this, we not only announce the kingdom, but we also practice for living in it; we not only long for it, but we also begin to enjoy it.

The Kingdom That Comes

Frequently, Christian hope is centered on the expectation of a place beyond this world where those who are saved enjoy eternal life. Certainly, eternal life is a fundamental part of God's promise, and its context is the kingdom of God. But when we pray "Thy kingdom come," we are not referring to a place where we are going but rather to a reality that comes to us. Due mostly to the influence of Plato and other philosophers after him, Christians often think in terms of a kingdom "up there" to which we go rather than in terms of a kingdom "out there" that comes to us. Doubtless, as we saw in the discussion of "heaven and earth" in chapter 3, created reality includes a vast sphere of the unknown. But it is not to this that we refer when we ask that God's kingdom will come. The kingdom of God isn't so much a place as it is a new order in which, as we shall see in the next chapter, the will of God is done. Although it's true that when Jesus is with us the kingdom is also present, it is also true that the fullness of the kingdom will not come until the final manifestation of Jesus and the fulfillment of the will of God both in the sphere of mystery that we call "heaven" and in the other that we do know and call "earth."

But we must take care when we speak of a heavenly kingdom and another on earth. Frequently, such phrases give the impression that the kingdom of God is elsewhere, "out there," and that the earth on which we live has little to do with it. But in Scripture the kingdom of God is both heavenly and earthly. In the book of Revelation, John declares that he saw not only a new heaven but also a new earth (Rev. 21:1). Quite often we speak of the kingdom of God as if it is only a place where we go when we die, rather than something that we expect to come in the future. But the prayer that the Lord taught us clearly says otherwise: "Thy kingdom come."

What we are calling for is not so much a different place as a different order. It is a new order in which, as Jesus promises, those who have been last will be first, those who have been oppressed will be free, and where instead of injustice and exploitation there will now be justice, freedom, and love. This is the order, which the prophets proclaim in metaphors, that does not seem apparent within the present order:

> The wolf shall live with the lamb,
>> the leopard shall lie down with the kid,
> the calf and the lion and the fatling together,
>> and a little child shall lead them.
> The cow and the bear shall graze,
>> their young shall lie down together;
>> and the lion shall eat straw like the ox.
> The nursing child shall play over the hole of the asp,
>> and the weaned child shall put its hand on the adder's
>> den.
> They will not hurt or destroy

on all my holy mountain;
for the earth will be full of the knowledge of the LORD
as the waters cover the sea. (Isa. 11:6–9)

He shall judge between many peoples,
and shall arbitrate between strong nations far away;
they shall beat their swords into plowshares,
and their spears into pruning hooks;
nation shall not lift up sword against nation,
neither shall they learn war any more;
but they shall all sit under their own vines and under their
own fig trees,
and no one shall make them afraid;
for the mouth of the LORD of hosts has spoken.
(Mic. 4:3–4)

This vision and promise involve both hope and terror. It's a frightening vision for those who enjoy the present order and don't wish things to change. As early as the late second century, Tertullian referred to some who prayed that the coming of the kingdom would be delayed. It's not clear whether they were asking for more time for sinners to repent or they simply wished for the kingdom to be delayed because they were enjoying the present order. Today many of us are so comfortable that we may not ardently desire the passing of this order and the coming of another of justice, peace, and love.

Tertullian himself, after mentioning these people who were praying for the delay of the kingdom, says,

Our wish is, that our reign be hastened, not our servitude protracted. Even if it had not been prescribed in the Prayer that we should ask for the advent of the kingdom, we should, unbidden, have sent forth that cry, hastening toward the realization of our hope. The souls of the martyrs beneath the altar cry in jealousy unto the Lord "How long, Lord, dost Thou not avenge our blood on the inhabitants of the earth?" for, of course, their avenging is regulated by the end of the age. Nay, Lord, Thy kingdom come with all speed [means] the [answered] prayer of Christians, the confusion of the heathen, the exultation of angels[;] for the sake of [this kingdom.] we suffer, nay, rather, for [its] sake . . . we pray![6]

It is for the coming of this kingdom, of this surprising order that undermines the present order that we selfishly enjoy, that we call when we pray:

Our Father who art in heaven, hallowed be thy name. Thy kingdom come. Thy will be done on earth as it is in heaven. Give us this day our daily bread. And forgive us our debts, as we forgive our debtors. Lead us not into temptation. But deliver us from evil. For thine is the kingdom, and the power, and the glory forever. Amen.

6

Our Father who art in heaven, hallowed be thy name. Thy kingdom come. **Thy Will Be Done on Earth as It Is in Heaven**. Give us this day our daily bread. And forgive us our debts, as we forgive our debtors. Lead us not into temptation. But deliver us from evil. For thine is the kingdom, and the power, and the glory forever. Amen.

A Petition That Affirms a Promise

We now come to the last of the three petitions that, according to Thomas Aquinas, are not petitions, strictly speaking, but rather affirmations of the promises of God that will be fulfilled in the future. Like the two previous petitions, this one, even though worded as if we were asking something of God, actually involves a commitment on our part. We are committed to act as those who know that the promises of God will be fulfilled in the future and that this knowledge calls us to certain actions and attitudes in the present. Just as when we ask that God's name be hallowed we don't claim that God should be made holier, now when we ask that the will of God be done we don't mean that there is any doubt it will be so.

Tertullian considers this petition so important that he discusses it even before the petition calling for the coming of the kingdom. His interpretation, which has been the most common throughout church history, is that we are really asking God to fulfill the divine will:

> What, moreover, *does* God will, but that we should walk according to His Discipline? We make petition, then, that He supply us with

the substance of His will, and the capacity to do it, that we may be
saved both in the heavens and on earth; because the sum of His
will is the salvation of them whom He has adopted.[1]

Likewise, during the Protestant Reformation John Calvin affirmed that this petition regarding the will of God is implicit in the
previous one regarding the coming of the kingdom and cannot be
separated from it, since

> [t]he third petition is: that God's will may be done on earth as in
> heaven. Even though it depends upon his Kingdom and cannot
> be separated from it, still it is with reason added separately on
> account of our ignorance, which does not easily or immediately
> comprehend what it means that "God reigns in the world." It will
> therefore not be absurd to take it as an explanation that God will
> be King in the world when all submit to his will.[2]

Thirteen centuries earlier, Cyprian had written eloquent words
regarding the meaning of this petition:

> Now that is the will of God which Christ both did and taught.
> Humility in conversation; steadfastness in faith; modesty in words;
> justice in deeds; mercifulness in works; discipline in morals; to
> be unable to do a wrong, and to be able to bear a wrong when
> done; to keep peace with the brethren; to love God with all one's
> heart; to love Him in that He is a Father; to fear Him in that He
> is God; to prefer nothing whatever to Christ, because He did not
> prefer anything to us; to adhere inseparably to His love; to stand
> by His cross bravely and faithfully; when there is any contest on
> behalf of His name and honour, to exhibit in discourse that con-
> stancy wherewith we make confession; in torture, that confidence
> wherewith we do battle; in death, that patience whereby we are

crowned; — this is to desire to be fellow-heirs with Christ; this is to do the commandment of God; this is to fulfil the will of the Father.[3]

The same may be seen in one of John Chrysostom's homilies on the Gospel of Matthew. Chrysostom comments,

Behold a most excellent train of thought! in that He bade us indeed long for the things to come, and hasten towards that so-journ; and, till that may be, even while we abide here, so long to be earnest in showing forth the same conversation as those above. For ye must long, saith He, for heaven, and the things in heaven; however, even before heaven, He hath bidden us make the earth a heaven and do and say all things, even while we are continuing in it, as having our conversation there; insomuch that these too should be objects of our prayer to the Lord. For there is nothing to hinder our reaching the perfection of the powers above, because we inhabit the earth; but it is possible even while abiding here, to do all, as though already placed on high. What He saith therefore is this: "As there all things are done without hindrance, and the angels are not partly obedient and partly disobedient, but in all things yield and obey . . . ; so vouchsafe that we men may not do Thy will by halves, but perform all things as Thou willest."[4]

Likewise at about the same time Augustine was preaching in similar terms,

We then add: Your will be done on earth as it is in heaven. The angels in heaven serve you; let us serve you on earth. The angels in heaven do not offend you; let us on earth not offend you. Let us do your will as they do it. So, what are we asking, if not that we may be righteous? When we do the will of God (for there is no doubt that God does God's will), then his will is done in us.[5]

Thus, ancient Christian writers seem to be in general agreement that the petition regarding the will of God is above all a plea that God will help us obey the divine will, as well as a commitment to do so.

Two Strange Interpretations

Despite general agreement on this interpretation, some ancient writers, apparently influenced by Platonic philosophy, interpret this petition by suggesting that the words *heaven* and *earth* refer to the duality in human nature, which is partly celestial and partly earthly. This appears as early as the third century with Cyprian:

> Moreover, we ask that the will of God may be done both in heaven and in earth, each of which things pertains to the fulfilment of our safety and salvation. For since we possess the body from the earth and the spirit from heaven, we ourselves are earth and heaven; and in both — that is, both in body and spirit — we pray that God's will may be done. For between the flesh and spirit there is a struggle; and there is a daily strife as they disagree one with the other, so that we cannot do those very things that we would, in that the spirit seeks heavenly and divine things, while the flesh lusts after earthly and temporal things; and therefore we ask that, by the help and assistance of God, agreement may be made between these two natures, so that while the will of God is done both in the spirit and in the flesh, the soul which is new-born by Him may be preserved.[6]

The same idea, with even stronger Platonic overtones, was expressed a century later by Gregory of Nyssa:

> The rational creation may be divided between the incorporeal and the corporeal. The first is typical of angels, and the second of us.

A spiritual creature, free as it is from the ballast of a body . . . dwells in the higher regions of ethereal light and moves freely. But this other nature is limited to our earthly life because it is tied to our body, which is a sort of sediment or muck. . . . A heavenly body is completely free of evil and the powers of evil have nothing to do with it. But in this lower life, where human nature resides, there are also all sorts of desires and passions. . . . Therefore this prayer teaches us to purify our life from all evil so that the will of God may rule in us with no impediment, as is true in heaven.[7]

In a word, when we pray that God's will be done on earth as it is in heaven, we are asking that the good impulses that are part of our heavenly nature, or soul, may also be felt in our earthly nature or body, so that God's will may be done in all our being.

No matter how inspiring this may sound, it involves two errors that soon took hold of much of Christian piety and theology, errors that we must avoid. The first is the suggestion that whatever evil there is in us resides in the body, while good reigns in our spirits. This is often supported by an interpretation of what Paul says about his inner struggles as a conflict between his good, purely spiritual, or celestial, being, and his material and earthly body (see Rom. 7:14–20). Such a view seems to forget that much of what is evil in us is not limited to the physical or corporeal. Sin is not simply a matter of allowing ourselves to be carried away by bodily impulses, as many seem to think, but also allowing ourselves to be carried away by the evil impulses in our souls. Hatred, envy, and other similar evils are not purely physical realities but dwell in the human spirit, as well — in what more Platonic interpreters such as Gregory of Nyssa would call our heavenly component.

The second error, completely without biblical foundation but quite common among many Christians, is to imagine that redemption has nothing to do with the physical world or with our bodies.

TEACH US TO PRAY

This view derives from both Greek philosophical thought and much
of the surrounding culture, but it is quite contrary to the biblical
understanding of the goodness of the entire human being as well
as of the entire creation — material as well as spiritual. At the very
beginning of Genesis we are told that God made the heavens and the
earth. The earth, and not only heaven, is God's creation and is therefore an object of divine love. Therefore, when we pray that God's
will be done on earth as it is in heaven we are not asking that earth
become a purely spiritual reality. We are asking rather that all things,
both in heaven and on earth, will be subjected to the will of God.

We can also find, although less frequently, another strange interpretation of this petition in the Lord's Prayer among ancient Christian writers. According to this interpretation, heaven and earth are a
metaphor representing believers and unbelievers. It may be found,
for instance, in both Cyprian and Augustine. Cyprian says that in
the Lord's Prayer we

> . . . pray and ask by the admonition of Christ as to make our prayer
> for the salvation of all men; that as in heaven — that is, in us by
> our faith — the will of God has been done, so that we might be
> of heaven; so also in earth — that is, in those who believe not —
> God's will may be done, that they who as yet are by their first
> birth of earth, may, being born of water and of the Spirit, begin
> to be of heaven.[8]

Augustine makes the same point, although now referring not so
much to believers as to the church itself:

> We can also see the church as heaven, for it has God within it, and
> earth as unbelievers, who have been told: "Earth you are, and to
> earth you will return." Thus, when we pray for our enemies — the
> enemies of the church, the enemies of the name of Christian — all

that we seek is that God's will may be done on this earth as it is in heaven, meaning that it be done in those who blaspheme as it is done in believers, and thus all may attain to heaven.[9]

The error here is that we all know that the church is no heaven and that its inner life is far from being heavenly. In the church there are all sorts of sin, just as there are in the rest of society. Without a doubt, when we pray that God's will be done, we are praying for the salvation of all. And it's also true that believers must pray for all who do not know the message of salvation. But the text itself, in speaking of heaven and earth, isn't dealing only with the salvation of individuals, or with the salvation of the church, but rather with the whole of God's creation. The heaven and earth in which God's will shall be done are the heaven and earth that God has created, both renewed by God's power.

God's Will and Ours

It's important to underscore, as do ancient Christian commentaries on the Lord's Prayer and most Christians throughout history, that when we ask that the will of God be done, we are ready to set aside our own will, placing God's above it. It is quite common among the commentaries on the Lord's Prayer to relate this particular clause with the prayer of Jesus in Gethsemane when he was about to be betrayed. According to the Gospel of Matthew, he prayed, "My Father, if it is possible, let this cup pass from me; yet not what I want but what you want" (Matt. 26:39). Commenting on this passage, Tertullian says that Jesus has given us a prime example of what it means to surrender to God's will: "[Jesus] Himself *was* the Will and the Power of the Father: and yet, for the demonstration of the patience which was due, He gave Himself up *to* the Father's Will."[10] And Cyprian adds, "Now if the Son was obedient to do His Father's will, how much more should the servant be obedient to do his Master's will!"[11]

This reminds us that the prayer that Jesus taught his disciples was also the pattern of prayer that he followed. He who had taught his followers to pray that the will of God be done above any other will, at the time of his terrible anguish in Gethsemane prayed just as he had taught his disciples: "My Father, if it is possible, let this cup pass from me; yet not what I want but what you want."

Therefore, the various authors whom we have quoted would agree that the clause we are now studying is not only something that we ask of God but is also a promise and commitment by which we are ready to be judged. When we ask that the will of God be done on earth as it is in heaven, we are offering God the obedience of our own wills.

What makes all this more difficult is that we know quite well that our wills are rebellious, that we constantly find ways to do what is convenient or attractive, setting aside the will of God. Although it's true that sometimes we don't know exactly what the will of God is, in general we know at least its parameters. As Cyprian says, the will of God is what Christ himself taught and followed.

Thus, when we ask that God's will be done on earth as it is done in heaven, even though we may not realize it, we are committing ourselves to an obedience that we will not be able to fulfill, and we are preparing the way for other petitions in this prayer that show our own disobedience and our debt before God. This is closely related to the petition that we will examine in the next chapter.

Heaven and Earth

However, before turning to that other petition we must return to a matter already discussed but that requires further clarification: what is the meaning here of the words *heaven* and *earth*? As we saw when we looked at the clause "who art in heaven," when we speak jointly of "heaven and earth," this does not refer primarily to two different realities, one in one place and the other in another, but rather to the sphere of the known or knowable on the one hand and the sphere of impenetrable mystery on the other. In this sense, the earth is not only the planet on which we live but includes also all that we may know or explore, from the farthest reaches of interstellar space to the most basic subatomic particle. When we use these two words together, we are affirming, as Barth says, that reality is not just the creation that we may know or understand. It includes heaven, which is not open to our scrutiny and understanding. Yet even this heaven is not God. There is no doubt that God is veiled in mystery. But when we say that God made the heavens and the earth, we affirm that God has made and is above both the reality that we can know and other realities far beyond the reach of our understanding or explanation.

Therefore, when we speak of the will of God being done in heaven, we are acknowledging that in some way that we can never understand or even suspect, the will of God is done in ways hidden from us. When we say that we expect the future kingdom, we do not imply that the will of God will not be done until that kingdom comes. We are asking, rather, that the will of God may be fulfilled in this world that we are able to understand — in the world of human relations, as well us in the world of atmospheric phenomena and outer space — just as by faith we know that it is being fulfilled in that which our minds are unable to understand. If the earth is that part of creation that we are able to know, then within that earth are some things that we can change and reorganize. But clearly, this power has limits. We know, for instance, what conditions produce hurricanes, but up to this day we haven't found a way to use that knowledge in order to avoid the destruction caused by hurricanes. However, conceivably, the day will come when such a thing will be possible. Perhaps, stressing our human capabilities to their limits, we may imagine that the time will come when we will know how to manipulate other phenomena. But even this would still be part of earth, and not of that heaven which is also God's creation. Consequently, when we ask that God's will be done on earth as it is done in heaven we are committing ourselves to take care of the earth as God wills. We are committing ourselves not to abuse creation or to exploit and destroy it for our own designs and pleasures.

That commitment certainly has personal dimensions — as Cyprian would say, "humility in conversation; steadfastness in faith; modesty in words." But there are also social or corporate dimensions to it — again, as Cyprian would say, "justice in deeds; mercifulness in works." Among the things that we can manage and organize, however imperfectly, is the society in which we live. The will of God is not being done when oppression or exploitation dominates that society, when the response to violence is even greater violence, or when thousands starve to death while others have more than they need. This will become clear as we look at the rest of the Lord's Prayer, and as we pray ever more earnestly,

> **Our Father who art in heaven, hallowed be thy name. Thy kingdom come. Thy will be done on earth as it is in heaven.** Give us this day our daily bread. And forgive us our debts, as we forgive our debtors. Lead us not into temptation. But deliver us from evil. For thine is the kingdom, and the power, and the glory forever. Amen.

7

Our Father who art in heaven, hallowed be thy name. Thy kingdom come. Thy will be done on earth as it is in heaven. **Give Us This Day Our Daily Bread**. And forgive us our debts, as we forgive our debtors. Lead us not into temptation. But deliver us from evil. For thine is the kingdom, and the power, and the glory forever. Amen.

Far-Reaching Implications

We now come to the first of the petitions in the Lord's Prayer in which those who pray, rather than just praising God and committing to obey the divine commandments, actually ask for themselves: "Give us this day our daily bread." This apparently simple petition has far-reaching implications for two reasons. First, early Christians tried to find other meanings in this petition beyond the ordinary bread that we eat each day. Second, what we ask for in saying these words has consequences that go far beyond what we commonly think. Let us deal first with the not-so-obvious interpretations in order then to turn to what the petition in its literal meaning actually implies.

Various Interpretations

As we have already seen, from an early date Christians began to refer to the Lord's Prayer in their writing, and they referred specifically to this petition. Interpreters generally agree that the bread of which Jesus speaks in this prayer has to do with the physical bread that nourishes us, as well as with all that it represents: physical sustenance, clothing, and so forth. But soon other interpretations were added to this one.

The most interesting of these interpretations should not surprise us if we remember that the church gathered at least once a week, on the first day of the week, to break bread — what today we call Communion or the Lord's Supper. Therefore, when worshippers raised this petition, they would immediately draw connections between the ordinary bread to which Jesus refers and the bread that the church was about to share in Communion. They easily made these connections since Jesus had spoken of himself as "the bread of life." These words appear in the sixth chapter of the Gospel of John where, after feeding the five thousand, Jesus says, "Do not work for the food that perishes, but for the food that endures for eternal life, which the Son of Man will give you" (v. 27). Then, after discussing the "bread from heaven" that God had given in the form of manna in the desert, Jesus ends his teaching by declaring that he is the bread of life and that those who come to him will never hunger. Therefore it was logical and easy, when the Lord's Prayer was said during Communion, to connect the petition for daily bread with the Communion bread that the congregation was sharing. Tertullian, after a few words about the daily bread, says,

> We may rather understand, "Give us this day our daily bread," *spiritually*. For *Christ* is our Bread; because Christ is Life, and bread is life. "I am," saith He, "the Bread of Life"; and, a little above, "The Bread is the Word of the living God, who came down from the heavens." Then *we find*, too, that His body is reckoned in bread: "This is my body." And so, in petitioning for "daily bread," we ask for perpetuity in Christ, and indivisibility from His body.[1]

Shortly thereafter Cyprian, who spoke of Tertullian as a great teacher to be imitated, wrote about this petition:

As the prayer goes forward, we ask and say, "Give us this day our daily bread." And this may be understood both spiritually and literally, because either way of understanding it is rich in divine usefulness to our salvation. For Christ is the bread of life; and this bread does not belong to all men, but it is ours. And according as we say, "Our Father," because He is the Father of those who understand and believe; so also we call it "our bread," because Christ is the bread of those who are in union with His body. And we ask that this bread should be given to us daily, that we who are in Christ, and daily receive the Eucharist for the food of salvation, may not, by the interposition of some heinous sin, by being prevented, as withheld and not communicating, from partaking of the heavenly bread, be separated from Christ's body.[2]

This way of relating the daily bread in the prayer to the bread of Communion and to the presence of Christ is a constant theme throughout ancient Christian literature, as well as in other interpretations to this day.

Origen, the Alexandrian scholar who became well known for his careful study of Scripture, always seeking in it profound meanings hidden in allegories and metaphors, was noted for his interpretation of the petition for daily bread. At the beginning of his commentary on this petition, Origen declares what he will do: "Some believe that in this prayer Jesus tells us to ask for bread for the body, but on the basis of what the Lord himself says about the bread, I can offer a different interpretation."[3] Origen says that the word that we now translate as "daily" is a Greek word unknown to him. In order to explain its meaning he goes into a study of the supposed etymology of the word, and this in turn leads him to stress the "spiritual" interpretation of this daily bread to which Jesus refers. The Greek word is *epiousios*. According to Origen, the authors of the Gospels, in translating the original words of Jesus into Greek, coined this new word. His etymological study leads him to the conclusion that the word itself is composed of two parts. One of them is *epi*, which means, among other things, "next to," "near," or "toward." The other is *ousia*, which means "substance" or "essence." Joining these two roots, Origen decides that Jesus is not speaking about the physical bread that nourishes the body but rather about the "supersubstantial" bread that nourishes believers.

Today we know that Origen was wrong when he claimed that the authors of the Gospels had invented this word and also when he supposed that it meant "supersubstantial" bread. The word *epiousios* appears in some ancient writings that Origen did not know, and it clearly meant *daily*. Apparently by the third century the word was no longer in common usage, and therefore Origen developed his faulty etymology. After that, particularly among some of the greatest scholars of antiquity, Origen's interpretation became common. Jerome, the erudite translator of the Latin Vulgate, following what Origen had said, translated the petition we are studying as, *Panem nostrum supersubstantialem da nobis hodie* — "give us today our supersubstantial bread." Similarly Ambrose, a scholarly fourth-century bishop of Milan who wrote in Latin but was well acquainted with Greek writings and theology, followed Origen's etymology. The old Latin version of Scripture that he used referred to "daily bread" — *panis cotidianus*, and Ambrose retained those words. But he still insisted that what Origen said was true, and that this daily bread was actually also the "supersubstantial" bread of Communion. On that basis, he criticized Greek-speaking Christians for not celebrating Communion as often as they should, for this supersubstantial bread of Communion is needed daily, just as ordinary bread is. Later, Augustine would follow the same path, stressing the need to partake of Communion every day and criticizing Greek monks for not doing so. But he then excused them because their Bible did not say "daily" but rather "supersubstantial."

Eventually, most ancient writers came to the conclusion that the petition actually referred to three different meanings of the word *bread*: first, the physical bread that nourishes people each day; second, that spiritual bread which is Christ and by which Christians are nourished in their worship; and third, the bread of the Word, which nourishes Christians every day. Augustine summarized what by his time had become the traditional trifold interpretation:

> The fourth petition is *Give us this day our daily bread.* The daily bread refers to [1] all the things that are necessary for sustaining present life . . . [2] or the sacrament of the body of Christ, which we receive daily, [3] or spiritual food. . . .
>
> If any wish to understand this saying as referring to the bread that is needed by the body or to the sacrament of the body of the Lord, they must also understand all three meanings, so that we may at once ask for the bread that our bodies need, the visible bread consecrated in the sacrament, and the invisible bread of the Word of God.[4]

Although throughout the centuries the two other interpretations and applications have also been present, in general, the emphasis has been on the literal meaning of the text, referring directly to the physical bread that nourishes the body. This is the interpretation that we will consider in the rest of this chapter.

Daily Bread

In this petition we ask God to give us the sustenance necessary for living. Here bread is not only the baked product usually bearing that name but also everything that is necessary for life. Thus, even today we speak of someone as a breadwinner, but by this we don't mean a person is earning the money necessary to buy just bread. A breadwinner also seeks to provide clothing, shelter, and other basic needs.

Asking God for daily bread is a discipline in what Jesus directed his disciples to do: not worry too much about tomorrow. In the Sermon on the Mount, very soon after the introduction of the Lord's Prayer, Jesus speaks of the birds of the air, who "neither sow nor reap nor gather into barns," and yet God feeds them (Matt. 6:26). The petition also reminds us of the parable that Luke records:

> Then he told them a parable: "The land of a rich man produced abundantly. And he thought to himself, 'What should I do, for I have no place to store my crops?' Then he said, 'I will do this: I will pull down my barns and build larger ones, and there I will store all my grain and my goods. And I will say to my soul, Soul, you have ample goods laid up for many years; relax, eat, drink, be merry.' But God said to him, 'You fool! This very night your life is being demanded of you. And the things you have prepared, whose will they be?' So it is with those who store up treasures for themselves but are not rich toward God."
>
> He said to his disciples, "Therefore I tell you, do not worry about your life, what you will eat, or about your body, what you will wear. For life is more than food, and the body more than clothing. Consider the ravens: they neither sow nor reap, they have neither storehouse nor barn, and yet God feeds them. Of how much more value are you than the birds! (Luke 12:16–24)

Looking at the prayer's petition in light of this parable, note, first of all, that the petition does not mean that physical bread is unimportant. On the contrary, Jesus says that bread is so important that God will provide it. Nothing here supports what we often hear — that bread or physical needs are to be dismissed. But at the same time the petition, joined with the other passages quoted, declares an absolute trust in God. Like the rich man in the parable, one who does not trust God will seek assurance for the future by heaping up riches. But, as the parable shows, the future is not in our hands, and therefore it is folly to try to ensure it by our own efforts. Neither the poor who have nothing nor the rich who seem to have everything are ultimately in control of their future. Each day we depend on God for our life and sustenance.

Looking at this petition more carefully, we note that it is very similar to another request that appears in Proverbs 30:

> Give me neither poverty nor riches;
>> feed me with the food that I need,
> or I shall be full, and deny you,
>> and say, "Who is the LORD?"
> or I shall be poor, and steal,
>> and profane the name of my God. (Prov 30:8b–9)

One who prays in this fashion asks not only for daily bread but also asks not to be given more than is necessary. Scholars point out that the words "the food that I need" also meant a soldier's daily ration. The prayer asks for that and no more. Furthermore, notice that this passage connects not only with the particular petition in the Lord's Prayer that we are now studying, which is almost a direct quotation from Proverbs, but also with other clauses in the Lord's Prayer. According to Proverbs, one who has too much forgets God, while one who does not have enough is forced to steal and in so doing profanes the name of God, not only because stealing is a sin but also because it corrupts and destroys the social fiber that must be a mark of the people of God. Thus, while earlier in the Lord's Prayer we asked that the name of God be hallowed, we are now acknowledging that the hallowing of the name of God is to take place not only in worship but also in the manner in which society is organized. God's name is hallowed when society is so ordered that no one needs to steal and no one has so much that he or she will forget God and even deny God's existence.

Reading what early Christians said about this petition in the Lord's Prayer, we notice a theme that appears repeatedly but seems to have been forgotten in later centuries: the difference between what is necessary and what is superfluous. *Necessary* is that without which life cannot be healthy and normal. Everything else is superfluous. Owning anything that is superfluous for us but necessary for others is practically the same as stealing, and therefore believers who already have the equivalent of their daily bread are expected to share the rest with those who are in greater need. Many ancient Christian authors make this point. Here is what just a few say.

In the *Didache* or *Doctrine of the 12 Apostles* — already quoted as one of the three main sources that we have for the Lord's Prayer — we find the following words:

> Do not be like those who are prompt to open their hand to receive and close it when it comes to giving. . . . You shall not reject the needy, but will share all things with your brother and will call nothing your own. If you share the eternal goods, shouldn't you share even more in those that are passing?[5]

In the following century, in the city of Rome, a prophet by the name of Hermas warned believers,

> Now, therefore, listen to me, and be at peace one with another . . . and do not partake of God's creatures alone, but give abundantly of them to the needy. For some through the abundance of their food produce weakness in their flesh, . . . while the flesh of others who have no food is corrupted, because they have not sufficient nourishment. . . . Give heed to the judgment that is to come.[6]

Roman law held that owning property included the rights to use, enjoy, and abuse it (that last an understanding that was strongly rejected by many Christian leaders). A few decades after Hermas, Clement of Alexandria seems to have been referring to this when he wrote, "I know well the liberty of use, but only so far as necessary. . . . And it is monstrous for one to live in luxury while many are in want."[7]

In the fourth century, the words of Basil of Caesarea echo what many others are saying. After declaring that "whatever is superfluous is to be distributed among the needy," he adds strong words:

> Who is a miser? Anyone who is not content with having the necessary. Who is a thief? Anyone taking what belongs to others. Why then do you not consider yourself a miser and a thief when you claim for yourself what only was given to you so that you may manage it? If one takes another's clothing he is a thief. Why should we give any other name to one who is able to clothe the naked and refuses to do so? The bread that you hoard belongs to the poor; the cape that you hide in your trunk belongs to the naked; the shoes that rot in your home belonged to those who have no shoes.[8]

These passages, and many others that could be cited, show that the ancient church understood that when we ask for daily bread we are also asking — following the pattern set by Proverbs — not to have abundance at the expense of the needy.

In Paul's Second Epistle to the Corinthians, where he asks his readers to contribute to the support of the poor in Jerusalem, the apostle shows a similar understanding of the prayer. There Paul refers to the manna God provided in the desert when God commanded the children of Israel to gather a certain amount per person, corresponding to "enough for that day" (Exod. 16:4) — which reminds us of the petition in the Lord's Prayer. Disobeying these instructions, some collected more than they should and others did not have enough. "But when they measured it with an omer, those who gathered much had nothing over, and those who gathered little had no shortage; they gathered as much as each of them needed" (Exod. 16:18). Using this as an example, Paul exhorts the Corinthians to share what they have with the needy:

> I do not mean that there should be relief for others and pressure on you, but it is a question of a fair balance between your present abundance and their need, so that their abundance may be for your need, in order that there may be a fair balance. As it is written, "The one who had much did not have too much, and the one who had little did not have too little." (2 Cor. 8:13–15)

Quite possibly this understanding of the need to share inspired the life of the earliest Christians as it is described in the book of Acts:

> Now the whole group of those who believed were of one heart and soul, and no one claimed private ownership of any possessions, but everything they owned was held in common. With great power the apostles gave their testimony to the resurrection of the Lord Jesus, and great grace was upon them all. There was not a needy person among them, for as many as owned lands or houses sold them and brought the proceeds of what was sold. (Acts 4:32–34)

Furthermore, the petition for daily bread, which is offered both by those who have no bread and those who do, reminds us that daily bread is not only the result of one's work but is also a gift of God. The petition also shows that those of us who have more than we need run the risk of pronouncing these words hypocritically. On this subject, Calvin says,

Yet those who, not content with daily bread but panting after countless things with unbridled desire, or sated with their abundance, or carefree in their piled-up riches, supplicate God with this prayer are but mocking him. For the first ones ask him what they do not wish to receive, indeed, what they utterly abominate — namely, mere daily bread — and as much as possible cover up before God their propensity to greed, while true prayer ought to pour out before him the whole mind itself and whatever lies hidden within. But others ask of him what they least expect, that is, what they think they have within themselves.[9]

Our Daily Bread

That is not all. When we say "our daily bread," who is doing the asking? Is it the same person who earlier said "Our Father"? As we saw with the very first words of the Lord's Prayer, saying "Our Father" has a very different meaning than saying "My Father." Christians pray as a faith community jointly addressing our common parent. Likewise, when I say "Give us this day our daily bread," I am not only saying that I wish to have or need bread, but I'm also praying as a member of a community that, as a single body, prays for bread.

Furthermore, recall that in this prayer the word *our* means that we are speaking not only for believers but also for the entire world. From its early beginnings the church saw itself as a priestly people — as Peter would say, a "royal priesthood." When it prays, the church does so not only on behalf of its members or itself, but also on behalf of humankind, presenting itself before God as a priest taking all before the throne of grace. Likewise, when we ask for "our daily bread" we are not asking only for ourselves, nor even for our sisters and brothers in the church, but for the entire human race, even those who may not know our Lord. Even though they do not know it, we are also asking that they may have their daily bread.

In short, this petition in the Lord's Prayer, like many others, is not only a prayer but also a commitment. When we say "Give us this day our daily bread," we commit to sharing that which we have that is superfluous, as well as to doing everything possible so that those who do not have enough may have more. When we share our daily bread we also hallow the name of God. In that sharing we announce the fulfillment of the promise implied in the words, "Thy kingdom come. Thy will be done on earth as it is in heaven."

Let us then pray once more:

Our Father who art in heaven, hallowed be thy name. Thy kingdom come. Thy will be done on earth as it is in heaven. Give us this day our daily bread. And forgive us our debts, as we forgive our debtors. Lead us not into temptation. But deliver us from evil. For thine is the kingdom, and the power, and the glory forever. Amen.

8

Our Father who art in heaven, hallowed be thy name. Thy kingdom come. Thy will be done on earth as it is in heaven. Give us this day our daily bread. **And Forgive Us Our Debts, as We Forgive Our Debtors.** Lead us not into temptation. But deliver us from evil. For thine is the kingdom, and the power, and the glory forever. Amen.

The Confession of Sin

Up to this point in the Lord's Prayer, we have not acknowledged our own sinfulness, nor have we claimed any responsibility for the disorder in which we live. The first three clauses were devoted to exalting God and the divine designs and to making a commitment to follow those designs. First we committed to hallowing the name of God through our actions and attitudes, then to living as those who truly expect the kingdom of God, and finally to placing our wills at the service of God's will. Then, in the fourth petition, we acknowledged our physical frailty and need by asking for our daily bread. We might also say that in the fourth petition we acknowledged that all that we have comes from God, from this very God who, at the opening of our prayer, we called "Our Father," whose name we hallow, whose kingdom we await, and to whose will we submit.

But things are not that simple. Sin stands between God and us. No matter how much we commit to hallow the name of God and to submit to the divine will, we don't do it. We are sinners, and by not confessing this fact we break down our communication with God. Therefore, in the fifth petition we confess that we are sinners or debtors before God. This has been a central tenet of Christianity throughout the centuries, and it is this that we acknowledge in the fifth petition.

Many in the ancient church noted the change in mood that comes with this petition. Tertullian says, "It was suitable that, after contemplating the liberality of God, we should likewise address His clemency. . . . The Lord knew Himself to be the only guiltless One, and so He teaches that we beg 'to have our debts remitted us.' A petition for pardon is a full confession; because he who begs for pardon fully admits his guilt."[1] Similarly, Cyprian declares that "After the supply of food, pardon of sin is also asked for, that he who is fed by God may live in God, and that not only the present and temporal life may be provided for, but the eternal also, to which we may come if our sins are forgiven."[2] And much later, Martin Luther, after commenting on the daily bread, would say that "our next petition is this: that He may forgive us our debts and not look upon the shameful and thankless way we misuse the benefits with which He daily provides us in such abundance."[3]

The Lord's Prayer is often called the model prayer, for it teaches us that anything we might ask for or say in our own prayers that is contrary to the Lord's Prayer is illegitimate. In this clause, Jesus makes it clear that even though we may be able to call God Father, and no matter how much we seek to hallow God's name and to praise God for innumerable blessings, we must remember that we are still sinners. All the authors quoted above, as well as many others, repeatedly remind us of this. Cyprian expresses it as follows: "Lest any one should flatter himself that he is innocent, and by exalting himself should more deeply perish, he is instructed and taught that he sins daily, in that he is bidden to entreat daily for his sins."[4] Cyprian draws a parallel between the petition for daily bread and the daily petition for forgiveness through confession of sin. We were and still are sinners, and there is no other alternative than to acknowledge it. With his usual eloquence, Chrysostom declares, "After taking away so great evils, and after the unspeakable greatness of His gift, if men sin again, He counts them such as may be forgiven."[5]

Debts, Sins, and Trespasses

This clause of the Lord's Prayer has several different wordings. As it appears in Matthew, the prayer says, "forgive us our debts," while in Luke it says, "forgive us our sins." The *Didache* agrees with Matthew on this point. But in English we have a further problem, because many churches say, "forgive us our trespasses." Apparently the origin of this third wording is to be found in Jesus's explanation in Matthew 6:14, where he says, "For if you forgive others their trespasses. . . ." In 1662, the *Book of Common Prayer* of the Church of England translated this clause as "forgive us our trespasses," thus using in the prayer itself the terminology that Jesus later uses in verses 14 and 15. For this reason, many of the churches and denominations stemming from the Church of England still say, "forgive us our trespasses." Clearly, what the text in Matthew means when speaking of debts is sin, which is understood as a debt to God. Also, since Jesus refers to debts as trespasses as well, any of the three possible translations would seem to be acceptable.

A long tradition, particularly in the Western church, understands sin as a debt. Although most commonly this is understood as a debt to God, sometimes it is interpreted as a debt to the devil, to whom the sinner is now beholden. In his treatise *On the Sacraments*, Ambrose writes,

> The debt is nothing else but sin. The reason why you find yourself in such conditions is that you have borrowed money from the wrong moneylender. This is what makes you a sinner. When you were born you were rich, for you were made after the image of

God. But now you have lost what you had, true humility, because by claiming your own rights you became poor, and as naked as Adam. Needlessly you have contracted a debt to the devil. You were free in Christ, but now you are a slave to the devil. The evil one had your letter of debt, but on the cross Christ destroyed it, eliminating your debt and returning you to freedom.[6]

This view became the norm in the West, particularly through the influence of Saint Augustine, who echoed Ambrose by declaring that "there is no doubt that the Lord calls sins debts."[7]

While this understanding of sin is found throughout Christian tradition, it has become particularly important in the Western church — that is, all the churches that are heirs to the ancient Latin-speaking church, including both Roman Catholic and Protestant churches. Later, as we examine the last of the petitions in the Lord's Prayer, we will see another emphasis that, although present in all Christian tradition, has become particularly marked in the Eastern churches.

In the West, this emphasis on sin also appeared in the work of Anselm of Canterbury, who lived during the late eleventh and early twelfth centuries. His brief but extremely influential writing, *Why God Became Human (Cur Deus homo)*, explained that the purpose of Jesus's incarnation, and particularly of his death on the cross, was to pay for the debt of human sin. Anselm believed that the purpose of human life was the contemplation of God, and therefore to withdraw from such contemplation, even if it was in order to look at the most sublime of the heavenly bodies, would be an enormous debt owed to God. Referring to sin as a debt that is added to the previous debt we owe to God for having created us, Anselm says, "When you give God something of what you owe, even if you have not sinned, you must not consider this as a payment for your debt, for all that you can do you already owe to God."[8] Thus, the debts to which the Lord's Prayer refers are an unavoidable element of the human condition, for which a payment must be made. Anselm's idea soon became so influential in the Western church that today many Christians think this is the only proper way to understand the doctrine of redemption.

The Parable of the Debtor

This petition regarding debts and debtors immediately brings to mind a parable in the eighteenth chapter of Matthew that ancient Christian writers repeatedly related to the Lord's Prayer. The parable itself says,

> For this reason the kingdom of heaven may be compared to a king who wished to settle accounts with his slaves. When he began the reckoning, one who owed him ten thousand talents was brought to him; and, as he could not pay, his lord ordered him to be sold, together with his wife and children and all his possessions, and payment to be made. So the slave fell on his knees before him, saying, "Have patience with me, and I will pay you everything." And out of pity for him, the lord of that slave released him and forgave him the debt. But that same slave, as he went out, came upon one of his fellow slaves who owed him a hundred denarii; and seizing him by the throat, he said, "Pay what you owe." Then his fellow slave fell down and pleaded with him, "Have patience with me, and I will pay you." But he refused; then he went and threw him into prison until he would pay the debt. When his fellow slaves saw what had happened, they were greatly distressed, and they went and reported to their lord all that had taken place. Then his lord summoned him and said to him, "You wicked slave! I forgave you all that debt because you pleaded with me. Should you not have had mercy on your fellow slave, as I had mercy on you?" And in

anger his lord handed him over to be tortured until he would pay his entire debt. So my heavenly Father will also do to every one of you, if you do not forgive your brother or sister from your heart. (Matt. 18:23–35)

In order to understand this parable, we need to understand the enormous difference between what the servant owed the king and what the other servant owed the first servant. The first amount owed to the king, ten thousand talents, would be sixty million denarii, which would be the equivalent of a worker's salary for sixty million days of work — or, in today's terms, several billion dollars. It would have been an unimaginable amount for those hearing the parable. In contrast, the amount the second servant owed to the first was equivalent to one hundred days of work. What the king forgave was six hundred thousand times larger than what his servant refused to forgive. This parable illustrates what Anselm would later say, that anyone's debt before God is such that no one is able to pay it. It also means that whatever someone else owes us, no matter how large the debt, it is minuscule when compared to our own debt before God.

Each of the earlier petitions in the Lord's Prayer involves a commitment on our part. When we pray that God's name be hallowed, we commit ourselves to keep the name of God holy. When we ask that God's kingdom may come, we promise to live according to the values of that kingdom. When we ask that God's will be done, we commit to placing God's will above ours. When we ask for our daily bread, we pledge not to require more than is necessary and to share the superfluous. Now, as we ask God to forgive our debts, those debts include not having fulfilled the commitments that we have made in the rest of the prayer. If we ask that God's name be hallowed, then whenever we do or say anything that profanes that name, we have contracted a debt before God. If we ask for the coming of the kingdom of God, then when we follow the values and principles of the present order above those of the promised one, we owe God a debt. If we insist on doing our own will even though we know it is against the will of God, then we have become debtors before God. If we hoard bread and other resources that God provides, then we are in God's debt. It is all this that we acknowledge when we say "forgive us our debts."

Now, affirming that we wish to be forgiven "as we also have forgiven our debtors," we commit to forgiving whatever others owe us. Thus, when we ask God to forgive our sins, we are also referring to our relationship with other people. We commit to forgive them not only in exterior and visible ways but also in our inner self, and we show this by praying for them. To forgive our debtors means also to pray for them. And if they do not forgive us, we still have to pray for them.

This is the only petition in the Lord's Prayer that Jesus explains immediately after teaching the prayer itself. He says it quite clearly: "For if you forgive others their trespasses, your heavenly Father will also forgive you; but if you do not forgive others, neither will your Father forgive your trespasses" (Matt. 6:14–15).

Further along in the same Sermon on the Mount in which he taught this prayer, Jesus again shows the connection between our willingness to forgive others and the hope that God also will forgive us:

> Do not judge, so that you may not be judged. For with the judgment you make you will be judged, and the measure you give will be the measure you get. Why do you see the speck in your neighbor's eye, but do not notice the log in your own eye? Or how can you say to your neighbor, "Let me take the speck out of your eye," while the log is in your own eye? You hypocrite, first take the log out of your own eye, and then you will see clearly to take the speck out of your neighbor's eye. (Matt. 7:1–5)

The word *debt* in the context of this prayer means much more than what we commonly mean by such a word. It certainly has to do with forgiving the financial debts that others owe us. But it also refers to any other sort of debt. It has to do with someone who spoke evil of us, or another person who somehow hurt us, or a third one who plans evil against us. It is these debts that we are committing to forgive at the same time that we ask God to forgive our own debts. And, what is most terrifying, we are asking God not to forgive us if we do not forgive others!

Debts and Worship

For this reason, Christian worship should always include a time for confession and another for reconciliation. As Christians have understood throughout the ages, the Lord's Prayer serves as a model shaping all our prayers, but it is also the foundation on which worship is built. The first clauses of the prayer are words of praise for the love and majesty of God. In them we affirm that God is our Father, we hallow God's name, we surrender our will to God, and we place provision of our daily sustenance in God's hands. Now, as we come to this petition about debts, we confess that while we praise and love God we also disobey God's commandments and that we are therefore debtors before God — or, in more traditional terms, that we are sinners. To speak of our debts is to confess them. We are declaring ourselves sinners and debtors before God.

Unfortunately, our worship services often seem to ignore this dimension of Christian faith. Nearly everything about our worship emphasizes praise, hope, and joy. Certainly praise and joy are essential elements in Christian worship and faith. But we praise a God whose fatherly love is shown in forgiving our debts and showing us favor. Our Christian faith is joyful because we know that, even in our sinfulness, God's love is still with us. If we do not confess our sin, our praise and joy will fall short.

Traditionally, confession has been expressed in Christian worship by having a moment in which we communally declare ourselves to be sinful and also have an opportunity to confess our various individual sins before God.

Also, the Lord's Prayer emphasizes a close relationship between God's forgiveness and our forgiving others. For this reason in the ancient church — and in many churches to this day — it was customary, after confession and the announcement of God's forgiving love, for believers to express their mutual reconciliation. In the ancient church this was shown through the kiss of peace. This was so important in the ancient church that Origen says that without the kiss of peace — and the reconciliation signaled by it — there is no true worship or communion. He complains that some people who are fasting refuse to give the kiss of peace to others worshiping with them: "How can a prayer be complete without the kiss of peace? How can anyone think that peace may be an obstacle in the service of the Lord?"[9]

Today's equivalent of the kiss of peace is sometimes called sharing the peace, and in its most common form, it's a time when believers shake hands and exchange words of love and reconciliation. At this time we forgive one another just as we ask God to forgive us. If we cannot reach out in peace and be reconciled to the brother or sister who has offended us, we must remember that we will be measured by the same measure that we now use.

Jesus made the connection between worship and reconciliation inescapably clear: "So when you are offering your gift at the altar, if you remember that your brother or sister has something against you, leave your gift there before the altar and go; first be reconciled to your brother or sister, and then come and offer your gift" (Matt. 5:23–24). Likewise, he left no doubt that our love must include not only our friends and fellow believers, but even our enemies, and that in loving our enemies we are imitating God: "You have heard that it was said, 'You shall love your neighbor and hate your enemy.' But I say to you, love your enemies and pray for those who persecute you, so that you may be children of your Father in heaven; for he makes his sun rise on the evil and on the good, and sends rain on the righteous and on the unrighteous" (Matt. 5:43–45).

The Joy of Forgiveness

Even though our own sinfulness makes confession difficult and uncomfortable, confession also has a dimension of putting profound trust in this God who forgives us as a loving parent and calls us to new life. When we approach our earthly mother or father and confess that we have done something wrong, it's difficult and even painful. But at the same time that we make that confession, we know that our parents love us; therefore, even while we are confessing, and even beyond our fear of well-deserved punishment, we have a basic trust in these loving parents and therefore a deep and abiding joy. This is also the nature of our confession before God. It certainly is painful. It shames us. But even in the midst of pain and shame, we are certain that God loves us.

In confession we also experience the joy of imitating God, as children of this loving parent. The Epistle to the Ephesians calls us to experience just this: "Therefore be imitators of God, as beloved children, and live in love, as Christ loved us and gave himself up for us, a fragrant offering and sacrifice to God" (Eph. 5:1–2). Today we may refer to a child as being "a chip off the old block," by which we mean that the child is very much like his or her parents. Our goal, as children of this Father whom we claim and to whom we pray, is to be like God by loving others just as God loved us.

This was beautifully expressed in the fourth century by Gregory of Nyssa, who said about this petition of the Lord's Prayer:

It is clear that this passage tells us that as we approach a benefactor we must also be benefactors. If we approach someone who is good and just, we also have to be good and just. Since God is merciful and loving, we too must be merciful and loving. And so in everything else. Since God is tender and benign, gives us good gifts and deals with all mercifully, all of this that we see in the very being of God we must voluntary bring into our lives. . . . An evil person cannot be a close friend of a good one. Someone who wallows in impure thoughts cannot be a friend of a pure person. Likewise a person lacking in mercy who however claims to come to God is far from the love that God requires. This also means that anyone who oppresses a debtor is moving away from the love of God by this sort of life. How can there be any communion between cruelty and goodness, between being loving and being unmerciful? . . . Therefore, anyone who wishes to approach the love of God must be rid of any such insensitivities. . . .

In a strange way, the order of things here seems to be reversed, because here we are not asking God that we might be imitators of the divine, but rather that God may imitate us. Just as imitating divine goodness is a true blessing, now we dare ask God to imitate us when we do something good. . . . We are asking that God do with us what we have done with others; that God imitate me, who serve him even though I am but a poor beggar and God is the sovereign ruler of the universe. We are saying to God, "I have forgiven my debtors, not collecting their debts. I heard their laments asking for forgiveness and I have sent them in peace. Now you do likewise."[10]

Gregory then celebrates the joy that this brings. Anyone who is a child of someone whom they love and admire will try to imitate that parent. Our faith and our love for God are therefore shown in our readiness to forgive our debtors and be reconciled with our enemies. There is no greater joy than knowing that, seeing our own mercy, God is also moved to mercy for us.

It is in that trust that we painfully and yet joyfully confess our sin and pray for forgiveness:

Our Father who art in heaven, hallowed be thy name. Thy kingdom come. Thy will be done on earth as it is in heaven. Give us this day our daily bread. And forgive us our debts, as we forgive our debtors. Lead us not into temptation. But deliver us from evil. For thine is the kingdom, and the power, and the glory forever. Amen.

9

Our Father who art in heaven, hallowed be
thy name. Thy kingdom come. Thy will
be done on earth as it is in heaven. Give
us this day our daily bread. And forgive us
our debts, as we forgive our debtors. **Lead
Us Not into Temptation**. But deliver us
from evil. For thine is the kingdom, and the
power, and the glory forever. Amen.

Temptation

Commonly we understand the word *temptation* as an invitation to evil. Therefore, we repeatedly say that the devil tempts someone, or that a seducer tempts another person, or that someone is tempted to break a diet by eating a piece of pie. But in this petition of the Lord's Prayer it is God who may lead us into temptation. This means that we must understand more clearly what temptation is. The word used in the original Greek means both an invitation to evil and a test. In school, an exam is also called a *test* or an opportunity to show what we know. On other occasions we say that a difficulty or a tough decision is a test of character. The word that appears in the Lord's Prayer can mean such a test, as well as what we commonly mean by a temptation. It is used repeatedly in the Bible when people are told not to put God "to the test." This doesn't mean that we are not supposed to invite God to do evil, which would be absurd, but rather that we shouldn't test God's fidelity. We see this in chapter 4 of Matthew, where we are told (v. 1) that Jesus was taken to the wilderness "to be tempted by the devil," and later (v. 7) Jesus tells the devil that "it is written, 'Do not put the Lord your God to the test.'" When the devil tempts us, he invites us to do evil, but in the words that Jesus quotes, when humans tempt God they put God to the test. There is, however, a close relationship between both meanings, for at the very beginning of this passage in Matthew we read that "Jesus was led up by the Spirit into the wilderness to be tempted by the devil." In other words, the devil tempts Jesus to do evil, but it is the Spirit who takes Jesus to the place where he will be put to the test. This seems to indicate that whenever the Evil One tempts a believer, that very temptation is also a test coming from God.

The verb used here, which in most English translations of the Lord's Prayer is *to lead*, means "to guide someone along the way." It is a verb that is used, for instance, in Luke 5:18 for the action of those who were carrying a paralyzed man on a bed. It is the same verb that appears also in Hebrews 13:11, where we are told that the blood of the sacrifices was "brought into the sanctuary." Thus, there is every reason to translate this petition as "lead us not into temptation." Obviously, this creates difficulties for many believers who are puzzled about how it is possible that God would tempt someone, as if God wished us to do evil. For this reason, from a very early time some translators used language that did not seem to blame God for the temptation itself. Thus, the ancient Latin translation of the Bible said "do not allow us to be led" — *ne nos patiaris induci*. But when Jerome, probably the most careful biblical scholar of his time, produced the Vulgate, he said "do not lead us" — *ne nos inducas*. Despite the popularity of the Vulgate, several sixteenth-century translators of the Bible preferred the old Latin version — perhaps because it did not seem to blame God for temptation — and therefore translated this petition as "do not allow us to be led into temptation" or something similar. Most modern English versions say "lead us not into temptation," "do not put us to the test," or similar words. The traditional Spanish version says "do not let us fall into temptation" — *no nos dejes caer en tentación* — which may be understood both as "do not allow us to be tempted" and as "do not allow us to fall when tempted."

Since it is the Spirit, God, who leads Jesus to the place where he is to be tempted, we may well pray today that this may not happen to us, that God will not lead us into temptation, as we say in the Lord's Prayer. But at the same time it is the devil who then tempts us, and therefore we must also ask God that when we are tested we have God's strength and protection.

We cannot be tempted by the devil if God does not allow and wish it. But at the same time, when we are tempted, God provides the strength and resources to resist. This is what Paul says in his First Epistle to the Corinthians: "God is faithful, and he will not let you be tested beyond your strength, but with the testing he will also provide the way out so that you may be able to endure it" (1 Cor. 10:13). Note that what Paul says here is that God provides both the test and the resources to respond to it.

Our Tests

What then are those tests or temptations to which God leads us and in which the Evil One finds an opportunity? In their broadest meaning, these temptations arise every time we face a decision. A young woman has to decide whether to opt for a career that will make her rich or for another whose attraction is in the service that she will be able to render others. An employee has an opportunity to rise within his company and increase his income, but he will do so by speaking ill of a colleague. An entrepreneur considers the economic advantages drawn from closing a factory and weighs them against the consequence of leaving hundreds unemployed. Someone has the opportunity to satisfy sexual desires in a way that is not appropriate. We learn that someone is speaking ill of us, and we have an opportunity to respond in kind. While shopping, we have to decide whether to buy cheaper coffee from a company that exploits those who grow it, or pay more for a different brand that is produced more justly. We receive a paycheck, and must decide how to use our money. The list would be interminable, for it involves every decision we make.

In a way, all of life is a test — or a series of tests by which our character is both shown and formed. Obviously, our character is shown in how we respond to the tests we face. That young woman who has to make a decision about her career shows whether she is an altruistic person or a selfish one. An employee who can move ahead by speaking ill of another and does not do so signals his integrity. One who has the opportunity to respond in kind to character attacks and does not do it is showing mercy. The entrepreneur who decides to close a factory in order to make more money, even though the result will be that hundreds of families will have no income, shows a lack of compassion. A person who succumbs to illicit sexual desires shows lack of control. One who buys more expensive coffee so that peasants in a distant country may eat shows a profound sense of justice. In brief, the decisions we make signal our values and our faith — or our lack thereof.

But at the same time, when we respond to the various tests that we meet in life our character is being shaped. The young woman who decides to opt for a career with lesser economic benefits but greater satisfaction in service to others will be learning the joy of serving. An employee who falsely speaks of a colleague is increasingly becoming a liar. A woman who knows that someone is speaking evil of her and refuses to respond in kind is practicing and learning forgiveness and mercy. The entrepreneur who decides not to close the factory in order not to impoverish the families of its employees is becoming an ever more merciful person. One who refuses to follow unlawful sexual appetites is learning how to control thoughts and desires. The shopper who buys coffee that is fairly produced and processed learns how to follow justice and practice mercy. The ways in which we decide to use our money will either accustom us to comforts and activities that will soon appear to be needs, or they will give us greater concern for others. In all of this, character is being shaped.

Part of the shaping of our characters is the creation of habits. A habit is a practice or attitude so often repeated that eventually it becomes almost automatic. Some years ago I began making coffee immediately upon waking up in the morning, and I still do. I've done it over and over, year after year. This has become such a habit that sometimes a few minutes after rising I don't even remember turning on the coffee machine. Something similar happens with character formation. If we repeatedly tell the truth, even when a lie would be more convenient, speaking the truth will become a habit. If, on the other hand, we learn to work our way out of difficult situations by lying, we become liars — that is, lying becomes a habit. In summary, a test not only shows our character but also shapes it.

This implies that when God tests us — or, as the Lord's Prayer says, leads us "into temptation" — we are being given the opportunity to shape ourselves. Since the prayer we are studying begins by speaking of God as Father, we may see a parallel between those tests to which God subjects us and what our parents do in order to help us grow. When I was very young, I began receiving a weekly allowance from my parents to use as I saw fit. My parents knew that there was a good chance that I'd squander the money, but they also knew that without that practice and that temptation, or test, I'd never learn how to handle money wisely. When a mother loans her son the keys to the family car, she knows that he will be exposed to danger, but she also knows that if she doesn't loan the keys to her son, he will never learn how to drive confidently and responsibly. When parents encourage a daughter to move to another city in order to continue her studies, they know that she will be exposed to a multitude of dangers and temptations, but they also know that if she doesn't learn how to face those dangers and temptations, she will never become a mature woman. Likewise our heavenly Father, to whom we address the prayer we are studying, knows that we are constantly exposed to danger and temptations, but it is through the experience of facing such dangers and temptations that we become people capable of an ever closer relationship with God. Thus, when God leads us into temptation, God is motivated by the same love that we may see in all the other blessings we receive. It is through meeting those tests that we are learning to be true children of God and that we are increasingly shaped into the divine image.

This Petition and the Rest of the Prayer

We often think of the Lord's Prayer as a series of distinct petitions. But throughout our study we have seen that all of these are interwoven. The tests and temptations to which we refer in this petition are closely related to everything else we have said in this prayer. All the examples given for this petition are somehow included in the first five petitions we have already discussed. We say "hallowed be thy name," and the believer who does not speak the truth, but rather gives false witness, is profaning the name of God — the name in which that believer has been baptized and therefore the name that should be hallowed in all of life. We say "thy kingdom come," and the young woman who decides to follow a less lucrative career, but one of greater service, is reflecting the values of the kingdom for which she prays. We say "thy will be done," and that other young man who learns to control his sexual impulses is responding to what he has committed to by saying "thy will be done." We say "give us today our daily bread," and the entrepreneur who decides to keep the factory open, even though this will produce less profit for him but will also ensure that the families of his employees will have income, is fulfilling the commitment that he makes when he asks for daily bread. We say "forgive us our debts, as we forgive our debtors," and the person who has been the victim of slander and refuses to respond in kind is fulfilling the commitment involved in that petition.

During all this, it is important to remember once again the significance of the word *Our* at the very beginning of the prayer. When we pray, it is not only we individuals who pray, but we are praying jointly with the entire people of God; and not only do we pray for the people of God, but also, since we ourselves are a priestly people, we pray for those who do not pray or believe in God. When we ask God not to lead us into temptation and, if we are tempted, that God will support and guide us, we are asking for this also on behalf of others. When we ask God to accompany us when we are being tested, we are also asking for this on behalf of the neighbor who speaks ill of us, of the merchant who robs clients, and of the corrupt politician who takes for personal use what in truth belongs to the people. No matter how strange and difficult this may seem, we are asking also that they not be tempted, and that, when they are tempted or tested, God will lead them.

Back to Confession

In the previous chapter we saw that the petition regarding forgiveness of debts also reminds us that we ourselves are debtors and sinners and are always in need of confessing our sin before God. The petition "lead us not into temptation" also confesses not only our personal sin but also the sinfulness and the weakness that are implicit in our own nature and that therefore shape the entire fabric of society. When we say "lead us not into temptation," we confess that we lack the strength and the character necessary to respond adequately to the tests to which God may subject us. We say that we do not trust ourselves. We admit before God that we're afraid of being weak and disobedient. We know, for instance, that, even though we have asked God to judge us with the same measure with which we judge others, and that God will forgive us in the same way in which we forgive our debtors, we don't always have the necessary mercy to forgive those who work to our detriment. It's precisely because we know that we may fail the test that we ask God not to lead us into it. But in confessing before God that we fear the test, we also imply that we know that by our own means we cannot overcome all the tests of life. We are remembering what Paul says, that the same God who tests us will also provide the way out. Thus, when we confess our sin we also — although not explicitly — affirm the love, mercy, and power of God, with whose help we can overcome the test.

Since prayer must be constant, we must repeatedly ask God not to lead us into temptation and, when we are tempted, not to allow us to fall. It's not a matter of thinking that, because we are believers, because we attend church, or because our lives are purer than those of others, we have the strength necessary to respond to all our trials. The passage from Paul's First Epistle to the Corinthians is preceded by a warning: "So if you think you are standing, watch out that you do not fall" (1 Cor. 10:12). The prayer that the Lord has taught us is also an affirmation and confession of our constant and repeated need of divine aid in all the trials of life.

This is why, following the instructions of that Lord, and acknowledging that in the very words that we say we declare ourselves guilty of sin and lacking in strength to resist, we dare say:

Our Father who art in heaven, hallowed be thy name. Thy kingdom come. Thy will be done on earth as it is in heaven. Give us

this day our daily bread. And forgive us our debts, as we for-give our debtors. Lead us not into temptation. But deliver us from evil. For thine is the kingdom, and the power, and the glory forever. Amen.

10

Our Father who art in heaven, hallowed be thy name. Thy kingdom come. Thy will be done on earth as it is in heaven. Give us this day our daily bread. And forgive us our debts, as we forgive our debtors. Lead us not into temptation. **But Deliver Us from Evil.** For thine is the kingdom, and the power, and the glory forever. Amen.

❧❧ ❧❧ ❧❧

Evil and the Evil One

We come now to the last of the seven petitions in the Lord's Prayer, "but deliver us from evil." This is the only petition that begins with the conjunction *but*. The Greek word used here implies a strong contrast with the preceding petitions. It would be as if an employee would say, "I don't want to be paid more, but I want to have more respect." Therefore, this last petition is placed in contrast with the previous one, in which we ask God not to lead us into testing or temptation. Therefore, this evil from which we ask to be delivered is the opposite of being led into temptation.

This contrast helps us understand the nature of the evil from which we wish to be delivered. When we say these words we're usually thinking of the evils we commonly fear — sickness, poverty, abandonment, the loss of loved ones, and many other similar ills. We fear such things and call them evil for good reason. But at the same time, when such things happen to us they become part of those tests or temptations to which we referred in the previous clause.

It's good to ask God to free us from such things, for after all, prayer must come from the heart, and there is no doubt that we feel threatened by those dangers and potential ills. Jesus himself, when facing the cross, asked the Father to have that bitter cup pass him by if possible (Matt. 26:39). Paul repeatedly begged God to take away what he enigmatically calls a thorn in his flesh (2 Cor. 12:7–8). God doesn't want us to be hypocrites, claiming that we are ready to receive such ills when in fact we aren't. But God does expect and demand that we understand that our main problem, that which we must really fear, is not difficulties and bad events or any other misfortune, but rather the very power of evil that can possess our lives — the evil that wishes us to fail when we are tested.

The Greek words traditionally translated as *evil* could also be understood as "the Evil One." Who then would be this Evil One from whom we wish to be delivered? Immediately we think of evil people who threaten us or conspire against us. We do well in asking God to deliver us from such people and their cabals. But the evil to which this prayer refers goes far beyond that. It is not someone else who may wish us ill, nor is it some unfortunate or painful event. The evil from which we ask to be freed is the very power of evil, and therefore this petition could be translated as "but deliver us from the Evil One," or simply as "but deliver us from that which is evil."

A traditional way to refer to this evil power is by speaking of the devil. Unfortunately, the devil has become an object of ridicule by depicting him as a red imp with a tail and horns. Nothing in Scripture warrants such a view. But there is much in Scripture — and in our own personal and social experience — that reminds us that there is indeed a power of evil. Evil is not just something we do but also something that has us bound, something from which we must be freed. Evil is not just a random occurrence. It has a logic of its own. Therefore, personalizing evil by speaking of the devil is not far off the mark.

Delivering and Liberating

The Greek verb used here for what we ask of God when we say "deliver us" implies much more than simply avoiding misfortune. Delivering may mean simply helping us avoid something we fear or deplore. We may be delivered from the fear of unemployment, or a slave may be delivered from the fury of a master. The mistreatment of a slave is evil and unjust. Even so, the slave needs not so much to be delivered from mistreatment as to be liberated from slavery. A bird in a cage needs food and water, and by providing it we deliver it from hunger and thirst. But what the bird needs is much more than that. It needs the cage to be opened so that it can fly. Likewise, when we ask to be delivered from that which is evil, we are not just speaking of avoiding pains and torments, nor even of preventing that which is evil from mistreating us. We are actually asking that we be liberated from a slavery to which we are subjected and from a wickedness that encages us.

To understand this we must remember that evil is much more than actions that we commit or sufferings that befall us. Although certain actions are properly called sins, sin in itself is much more than such actions. Sin is a slavery to which we are subjected, a cage that does not allow us to live freely to follow the designs of the Lord. Therefore, when we ask to be delivered from the Evil One, we are not simply asking that we be able to avoid pain and sorrow. We are also asking that we be restored to a freedom we do not have.

In an earlier chapter we saw that, while in the West sin most commonly came to be understood as a debt before God, in the Greek-speaking East sin was viewed as a sort of slavery in which the Evil One holds us in subjection. Naturally, these two emphases are not mutually exclusive. On the contrary, while the Eastern church commonly referred to sin as slavery, it also saw sin as a debt before God.

Likewise, although the Western church stressed sin as a debt, there was always the vision of sin as a sort of slavery under which the Evil One holds humanity. Thus, even Anselm of Canterbury, in *Why God Became Human,* a work that has become the epitome of the emphasis on sin as a debt and on redemption as payment for that debt, also says that it was necessary for the Word of God to come in Jesus Christ, because humanity had to honor God "by overcoming the Demon, just as it injured God by being overcome by the Demon."[1]

Both slaves and birds in a cage have some measure of freedom. If they forget their slavery or their cage, they may well come to the point where they convince themselves that evil is a whip or a lack of proper food. Perhaps, since their lack of freedom becomes a daily experience, they may even come to the conclusion that theirs is a natural and inevitable condition. But the evil they suffer goes far beyond any ill that may befall them. Evil is much more than a bad experience, no matter how painful. Humans are under the slavery of that which is evil to such an extent that no matter how much we desire to do good we still are slaves of evil. It is to this that Paul points in a well-known passage:

> For we know that the law is spiritual; but I am of the flesh, sold into slavery under sin. I do not understand my own actions. For I do not do what I want, but I do the very thing I hate. Now if I do what I do not want, I agree that the law is good. But in fact it is no longer I that do it, but sin that dwells within me. For I know that nothing good dwells within me, that is, in my flesh. I can will what is right, but I cannot do it. For I do not do the good I want, but the evil I do not want is what I do. Now if I do what I do not want, it is no longer I that do it, but sin that dwells within me.
>
> So I find it to be a law that when I want to do what is good, evil lies close at hand. For I delight in the law of God in my inmost self, but I see in my members another law at war with the law of

my mind, making me captive to the law of sin that dwells in my members. Wretched man that I am! Who will rescue me from this body of death? (Rom. 7:14–24)

Irenaeus refers to slavery when he affirms that without the redemptive work of Jesus Christ humanity would have remained forever subject to sin, the presence and power of which would be endless and irremediable. Furthermore, according to Irenaeus, this subjection was so powerful that God introduced death in order to free humankind from eternal life under such conditions. In the face of such slavery, what is a great victory, or who is a champion who will destroy the power that the Evil One has over us? This is what the author of Ephesians means when he declares that Christ's incarnation, ministry, death, burial, resurrection, and ascension are a great work of liberation:

> Therefore it is said,
>   "When he ascended on high he made captivity itself a captive;
>   he gave gifts to his people."
> (When it says, "He ascended," what does it mean but that he had also descended into the lower parts of the earth? He who descended is the same one who ascended far above all the heavens, so that he might fill all things.) (Eph. 4:8–10)

Joining this to what was said much earlier about the wide scope of the "we" for whom we pray "Our Father," we come to the conclusion that when we say "deliver us from evil" — or, perhaps more precisely, "deliver us from the Evil One" — we are not only asking God that we may be able to avoid difficulties, pain, and grief, but we are also and above all saying that we long for the time when "the creation itself will be set free from its bondage to decay and will obtain the freedom of the glory of the children of God" (Rom. 8:21).

Promise and Reality

Clearly, this total freedom from evil for which we are praying will take place only in the final day, when all the promises of God are ful-filled. As long as we are in this world, we will not only be tempted, but we will also be, at least in part, subject to the power of that which is evil. But at the same time, note that this prayer is not only for the future but also for the present. The entire Lord's Prayer has a future dimension from the very beginning, where we ask that God's kingdom come. But it also has a present dimension. It is now that we are to forgive our debtors. It is now that we need our daily bread. And it is also now that we have a foretaste of the freedom of the children of God. The struggle goes on, but by reason of our union with the Lord who has conquered evil and death we may live as those who enjoy the promise of this future victory. We have that foretaste of the future when we discover that, thanks to God's grace, we can forgive those who offend us. We enjoy that foretaste when our brothers and sisters forgive us. We enjoy that foretaste when we share our daily bread with the needy. Therefore, this prayer that is both a petition and a word of trust in a better future is also a sign of our present participation in that future joy. And this last petition, like the rest, besides being a petition, is also a commitment. We are committing ourselves to live in such a way that our lives point to our victory over that which is evil, not because we are strong, firm, or virtuous, but because our Lord is.

Back to Confession

As in the case of many other petitions of the Lord's Prayer, this one is also a confession. In asking God to deliver us from the power of that which is evil, we are also confessing that we are so enslaved that we share the experience of Paul of not being able to do the good that we wish and yet doing the evil we do not wish. The first step in reaching our liberation from the power of evil is to confess our inability to free ourselves from it.

This confession of our own weakness closes the series of petitions in the Lord's Prayer, and it closes them on a high note, for it announces the glorious freedom to which Paul refers. But at the same time it closes them on a low note, for it repeatedly reminds us of the frequency with which we do the evil that we do not wish and cease to do the good that we do wish. This is true not only of this final petition in the Lord's Prayer but also of every confession of sin. We don't confess our sin because we believe that God hates us but because we know that God, in divine grace, is ready to forgive us and shape us into the divine image.

Back to "We"

While we confess our sinfulness and call for our liberation in this last petition, we must not forget that throughout this prayer it is not *I* asking for myself, but rather a vast *we* that certainly includes the individual but also all those who this very day and through the ages raise and have raised to heaven this model prayer. And the petition includes not only me and my sisters and brothers in the faith but also the much greater *we* that is the entire creation. The power of evil is not limited to the individual sinner, but it also corrupts society as a whole and even creation itself. Paul declared this in a radical statement:

> I consider that the sufferings of this present time are not worth comparing with the glory about to be revealed to us. For the creation waits with eager longing for the revealing of the children of God; for the creation was subjected to futility, not of its own will but by the will of the one who subjected it, in hope that the

TEACH US TO PRAY

creation itself will be set free from its bondage to decay and will obtain the freedom of the glory of the children of God. We know that the whole creation has been groaning in labor pains until now; and not only the creation, but we ourselves, who have the first fruits of the Spirit, groan inwardly while we wait for adoption, the redemption of our bodies. (Rom. 8:18–23)

It is therefore with deep sorrow yet even deeper joy, in a spirit of victory even while knowing that we are vanquished, trusting this Father of ours to whom we pray, that we dare to say and rejoice in saying,

Our Father who art in heaven, hallowed be thy name. Thy kingdom come. Thy will be done on earth as it is in heaven. Give us this day our daily bread. And forgive us our debts, as we forgive our debtors. Lead us not into temptation. But deliver us from evil. For thine is the kingdom, and the power, and the glory forever. Amen.

I I

Our Father who art in heaven, hallowed be
thy name. Thy kingdom come. Thy will
be done on earth as it is in heaven. Give us
this day our daily bread. And forgive us our
debts, as we forgive our debtors. Lead us not
into temptation. But deliver us from evil.
**For Thine Is the Kingdom, and the Power,
and the Glory Forever**. Amen.

Textual Problems

The Lord's Prayer ends with a doxology, or formula of praise: "For thine is the kingdom, and the power, and the glory forever." Most of us have probably noticed that while Protestants generally include this doxology as part of the prayer itself, Roman Catholics end the Lord's Prayer with the petition "deliver us from evil." The origins of this difference are lost in the shadows of history. Long before any disagreements arose between Catholics and Protestants, many ancient texts already included this doxology and others did not. The most important ancient manuscripts of the New Testament that we have, which come from the fourth century, do not include it. Two of these are the manuscripts called Sinaiticus (because it was discovered on Mount Sinai) and Vaticanus (because it is kept in the Vatican library). However, the doxology itself does appear in slightly later manuscripts, such as the Washington manuscript from the fifth century. But much more important than this manuscript tradition is the fact that the text of the Lord's Prayer that appears in the *Didache*, which dates from late in the first century or early in the second, does include it — although the words that it uses are not exactly the same as those that we have today in the Gospel of

Matthew. The *Didache* closes the prayer with the words, "For thine is the power and the glory forever."

Most of the ancient authors that we have been following — Tertullian, Cyprian, Origen, and Augustine — do not include the doxology in their commentaries on the Lord's Prayer. But John Chrysostom, writing roughly at the same time as Augustine, does know it, for preaching on the Lord's Prayer he says,

> Having then made us anxious as before conflict, by putting us in mind of the enemy, and having cut away from us all our remissness; He again encourages and raises our spirits, by bringing to our remembrance the King under whom we are arrayed, and signifying Him to be more powerful than all. "For Thine," saith He, "is the kingdom, and the power, and the glory."[1]

Furthermore, ancient translations of the prayer into Syriac and Coptic do include the doxology. Although the Vulgate does not either, it does appear in other ancient Latin translations.

The situation is further complicated because in ancient times many felt that this prayer should be taught only to those who had been baptized, and therefore they felt a certain reluctance to write it down lest it be used unworthily. We have an example of this in the *Apostolic Tradition* of Hippolytus, which includes all sorts of formulas, but not the Lord's Prayer. Some interpreters think that a reference in that document to a "white stone" that is given to the baptized, and which certainly refers to things that the neophytes have not been allowed to know earlier, is — or at least includes — the Lord's Prayer. About such things, Hippolytus instructs that "let not unbelievers know it, until they are baptized: this is the white stone of which John said: 'There is upon it a new name written, which no one knoweth except he that receiveth the stone.'"[2]

In summary, all this indicates that the doxology itself is ancient, although it is impossible to know whether it originally appeared in the text of the Gospel of Matthew.

We do know that in ancient times it was customary to use this doxology or a similar one at the end of a series of prayers. Apparently, since the prayer that Jesus taught his disciples was the model that all other prayers followed, often a time of prayer began with the one taught by Jesus, up to the final petition, then included other petitions and words of praise, and closed with the doxology that is now part of our Lord's Prayer. In this way, all petitions to be raised that would normally relate more closely to specific situations and to the particular needs of the congregation would follow the parameters established by the model prayer that Jesus taught his disciples. This practice still continues in the worship of several churches, both in the East and in the West.

For

No matter whether it was part of the original text or not, this doxology, while rendering glory to God, reminds us that all we have said and asked for is based on the fact that the kingdom, the power, and the glory belong to God. For this reason the doxology begins with the word *for*. We pray thus because of the power and glory of God, by which God is sovereign not only above us who believe but also above all humankind and all creation.

In the passage from Chrysostom quoted above, he continues commenting on this doxology:

> Doth it not then follow, that if His be the kingdom, we should fear no one, since there can be none to withstand, and divide the empire with him. For when He saith, "Thine is the kingdom," He sets before us even him, who is warring against us, brought into subjection, though he seem to oppose, God for a while permitting it.[3]

Calvin echoes the same view:

> Moreover, there is added the reason why we should be so bold to
> ask and so confident of receiving. Even though this is not extant in
> the Latin versions, it is so appropriate to this place that it ought not
> to be omitted — namely, that his "is the Kingdom, and the power,
> and the glory, forever."[4]

Thus, both Chrysostom and Calvin see this doxology not only as
an appropriate way to end prayer with praise to God but also as the
foundation of an entirely different vision that believers should have
of themselves and their place within creation. Calvin, who is reluc-
tant to speak too highly of humans and our capabilities, points out
that even despite our iniquity we dare pray precisely because of what
we say in this doxology. The passage quoted above continues,

> This is firm and tranquil repose for our faith. For if our prayers
> were to be commended to God by our worth, who would even
> dare mutter in his presence? Now, however miserable we may be,
> though unworthiest of all, however devoid of all commendation,
> we will yet never lack a reason to pray, never be shorn of assurance,
> since his Kingdom, power, and glory can never be snatched away
> from our Father.[5]

This differs somewhat from Chrysostom's view, for he, as well
as most Eastern theologians, has a more positive view of human
possibilities and abilities than does Calvin. Therefore, Chrysostom
sees in this final doxology a sign of God's willingness to share divine
power and glory with humankind:

> "And the power," saith He. Therefore, manifold as thy weakness
> may be, thou mayest of right be confident, having such a one to

reign over thee, who is able fully to accomplish all, and that with ease, even by thee.

"And the glory, for ever. Amen." Thus He not only frees thee from the dangers that are approaching thee, but can make thee also glorious and illustrious. For as His power is great, so also is His glory unspeakable, and they are all boundless, and no end of them.[6]

In other words, when we close our prayer with these words, we are not only giving God the glory and honor, but are also rejoicing in a gift far beyond our comprehension, for we can't understand how God can clothe our miserable condition in a reflection of the glory and honor that forever belong only to God.

At the same time, it's important to stress that this doxology is the foundation for the entire prayer. We are able to pray as we do because the kingdom, the power, and the glory belong only to this our Father to whom we pray. If it were not so, our prayer would be in vain. But because it is so, our prayer is efficacious, and we can confidently pray,

> **Our Father who art in heaven, hallowed be thy name. Thy kingdom come. Thy will be done on earth as it is in heaven. Give us this day our daily bread. And forgive us our debts, as we forgive our debtors. Lead us not into temptation. But deliver us from evil. For thine is the kingdom, and the power, and the glory forever. Amen.**

12

Our Father who art in heaven, hallowed be
thy name. Thy kingdom come. Thy will
be done on earth as it is in heaven. Give us
this day our daily bread. And forgive us our
debts, as we forgive our debtors. Lead us not
into temptation. But deliver us from evil.
For thine is the kingdom, and the power,
and the glory forever. **Amen**.

Amen

This little word that we repeat so often without even thinking about it has a long history of profound significance. Although Hebrew in origin, this word passed into Greek mostly because the Septuagint — an ancient translation of the Hebrew Bible into Greek — sometimes preferred not to translate it but simply to transliterate it into Greek letters. (I say "sometimes" because in other cases the Septuagint translates the same Hebrew word as *truth*, *truthful*, or other similar words.) Since the Septuagint was the version of the Hebrew Bible that almost all the authors of the New Testament used, the word *amen* passed from the Septuagint both to the New Testament and to Christian worship and devotion. Note, however, that in some cases where the Greek text says "amen" modern translations also use words like "truly." See for instance Matthew 6:2: "Truly I tell you." This translation of the word has become necessary because in common usage *amen* has come to mean only "let it be so" or "I agree," whereas in ancient times it was also used to affirm an absolute declaration. It is used this way in Revelation 3:14: "The words of the Amen, the faithful and true witness, the origin of God's creation." Here the word itself is an unquestionable affirmation of the truthfulness of the Lord — a truthfulness so great that he can also be called the Truth.

This all means that when we say "amen" at the end of the prayer, we are not only saying "let it be" but also "thus it is" and "thus it shall be." Therefore, the word itself does not mean only agreement and hope but also commitment. When we say "amen," we are declaring our hope. But since the same word also means "thus it is," we are also declaring our commitment.

Therefore, we may well say that when we close our model prayer — as well as any other prayer — with the word *amen*, we are affirming not only our petitions and our wishes but also a reality that goes far beyond what our eyes can see, as well as the commitment implied in the petitions themselves. Throughout our study we have seen that each of the seven petitions in this prayer also implies a commitment on the part of those who speak them. Now, as we close our prayer saying "amen," we are expressing an unshakable hope based on our knowledge that this Father to whom we address our prayers is the same to whom forever belong the kingdom, the power, and the glory. And we are also saying that we are so certain that it is so that we are committing ourselves to it.

This second meaning of the word *amen* is like signing a legal document or taking a formal oath. A politician may write or say many things without being too concerned about the consequences. We do likewise. But when we are asked to sign what we have written, or when a politician is before a court under oath, the matter is much more serious. What we have written and must now sign is no longer a series of dreams or empty promises. What one says under oath is no longer words that the wind carries away. Likewise, when we close our prayer by saying "amen," we affirm a covenant with God, committing ourselves to all that we have just said.

We have said, "Hallowed be thy name," and thereby we are committed to behave in a way that sanctifies and glorifies God. We have said, "Thy kingdom come," and thereby have committed ourselves to live according to the values of the kingdom. We have said, "Thy will be done on earth as it is in heaven," and thereby we have committed to place God's will above ours. We have said, "Give us this day our daily bread," and thereby we are committed to trusting God for our sustenance and not to take the sustenance of others. We have said, "Forgive us our debts, as we forgive our debtors," and thereby are committed to forgiving our enemies and those who offend us. We have said, "Lead us not into temptation," and thereby we have confessed our own weakness and affirmed our commitment to resist temptation with God's help. We have said, "But deliver us from evil," and thereby are committed to living according to the glorious freedom of the children of God. And now we reaffirm all of this with a firm "Amen," which means not only "let it be so" but also "it is thus" and "thus it shall be" with God's help.

It is with that help that once again and each day of our lives we rejoice, saying:

> Our Father who art in heaven, hallowed be thy name. Thy kingdom come. Thy will be done on earth as it is in heaven. Give us this day our daily bread. And forgive us our debts, as we forgive our debtors. Lead us not into temptation. But deliver us from evil. For thine is the kingdom, and the power, and the glory forever. Amen.

Let it be! Amen! Thus it is! Amen! Thus it shall be! Amen!

For Reflection and Discussion

Uses of the Prayer in the Early Church

1. Does it surprise you that there are two different versions of the Lord's Prayer in the New Testament, and that there is still a third one in some of the earliest Christian literature? Why do you think the rendition in the Gospel of Matthew has become the best known?

2. The early church had certain hours set aside for daily prayer, and likewise, many believers today have set aside a time of day that they devote to prayer and study of Scripture. Usually we do this in private, but in the early church people gathered for such hours of prayer. Does your church have prayer services at which people gather just to pray? What reasons, good or bad, have led us to abandon setting aside times of communal prayer? Is it possible to organize something like prayer groups through social media? What would be their value? What problems do you see along the way?

3. The Lord's Prayer is often called the model for all prayer. How is this expressed in the worship of our churches? Is this really a prayer guiding every other prayer, or is it just a traditional way to close our liturgical prayers? How could this prayer serve as a model for your

own private prayer? Could this prayer help in developing personal or family devotions?

Chapter 1

1. Do you use the Lord's Prayer in your personal prayers? When you begin by saying "Our Father," in whose name are you praying? Do you ever say "our," when in fact you mean "my"? How does the emphasis on the plural "our" give the prayer a wider meaning?

2. What do you think about the quote from John Chrysostom (see page 24) on the effect that the Lord's Prayer has (or should have) on our understanding of the social order? Is it true? How do you see this in our own life?

3. What connection is there between the very first word of the Lord's Prayer, "our," and the universal priesthood of believers? What does this add to our traditional understanding of that priesthood? What does it tell us about the meaning of baptism? How could this understanding of the priesthood of all believers affect your private prayers? How could it affect communal prayers in worship?

Chapter 2

1. Does it surprise you that you can claim God as your Father? If so, how? If not, why not?

2. Does the word *Father* really convey to you a closeness to God? If you are a man who has children, do they usually address you as "father"? Is there a better way for us today to express the ancient word *Abba*?

3. Does the masculine *Father* upset you? Have you ever seen it used in order to promote male supremacy over women? What other alternatives do you see? What are the pros and cons of each of them?

4. What functions of an earthly parent reflect the parenthood of God? Loving? Feeding and sustaining? Defending? Correcting and chastising? How does the very act of creation reflect God's loving parenthood and how we relate to God?

Chapter 3

1. What comes to mind when you say, "Who art in heaven"? What is heaven? Is it a place? Is there any place where God is not present? Are there places or occasions in which the presence of God is particularly felt or in which God is particularly active in a special way?

2. How do you understand the relationship between heaven and earth? When the two words are placed together (as in "maker of heaven and earth"), what does each of them mean? How does this relate to the doctrine of creation?

3. When you look at Solomon's prayer at the dedication of the first temple (1 Kings 8:27–30), what do you think it means to have specific places where God has promised to be present — or to listen to us? Is Jesus such a "place"? Where do we see Jesus now?

Chapter 4

1. The word *hallowed* is not one we use in our daily lives. What do you mean by it when you repeat it in the Lord's Prayer?

2. If God is perfectly holy, why do we ask that God's name be hallowed? If nothing can detract from the holiness of God, and if profaning is the opposite of hallowing, what do we mean when we say that something profanes the name of God? What are some things that profane the name of God? What in your own lifestyle and society can profane the name of God?

3. In this chapter you have read that "when properly understood, holiness leads us to admiration, awe, and even terror" (see page 67). Is this true? How can the holiness of the God whom we have just called Father terrify us? What does this have to do with our surprise — or lack of it — at being able to call God *our* Father?

4. How does your own holiness relate to the hallowing of God's name? What relationship do you see between holiness and purity or virtue? Does one become holier by being better? Or is the reverse true: that one becomes better by being holier? What does this have to do with the difference between being holy and being "holier than thou"?

5. In baptism we have been set apart as a people called to holiness in order to reflect God's holiness to the world. What does this mean for the holiness of the church? If we think we are purer and more devoted than others in our church, does this justify our leaving that church in order to create a holier church?

Chapter 5

1. When you think about the kingdom or reign of God, do you think in terms of something that is already here that we must discover, or do you think also in terms of a promised future? How is

it that Jesus tells us that the kingdom is already among us but then also commands us to pray for the coming of the kingdom?

2. When you imagine the kingdom of God, which of these words are foremost in your mind: joy, justice, love, peace, reward, punishment, community, eternal life? Any others?

3. Sometimes we speak of "building the kingdom of God" and of "bringing in the kingdom." Can we really build or bring about the kingdom of God? What is right and what is wrong about these expressions?

4. How do you understand the parables in which Jesus speaks of the kingdom as yeast in dough or as a small mustard seed? Think about the "great reversal" mentioned in this chapter (see pages 83–84). Is this a proper understanding of some of the parables of Jesus? If so, what does it mean for our life in the present order? How can we serve such a kingdom today?

5. Where have you seen glimpses of the kingdom in recent days? Have you seen them in your personal life? Have you seen them in others? In the news?

Chapter 6

1. Thomas Aquinas says that the petition "Thy will be done on earth as it is in heaven" and the two preceding it are not petitions in the strict sense but also declarations of our commitment to the hallowing of God, to living life according to the coming kingdom, and to doing the will of God. Is this true? When you use this phrase, are you simply asking God to do something, or are you also committing to take part in God's action?

2. In this petition we find again the terms *heaven* and *earth*, which were discussed earlier. Do you understand these as two different places, so that God's will is done "up there" but not "down here"? Or do you understand them as two different orders, so that wherever God's will is done heaven is present, and wherever it is not done is earth? How do you reconcile this thinking with the biblical affirmation that God is the maker of both heaven and earth?

3. Some people understand heaven as referring to things spiritual and earth as having to do with the physical world. What consequences does this have for our Christian life? Are they good?

4. How in your own life or in the life of the church do you see the struggle between following your own will and following the will of God? How do you learn the will of God?

Chapter 7

1. When we ask for daily bread, what sort of bread are we asking for? Are we asking only for bread or also for the other necessities of life? What are these necessities? Early Christianity made a clear distinction between what is necessary and what is superfluous. Is that distinction still valid for us today? What does this have to do with the subject of stewardship and the management of resources?

2. In our consumer society many seek to live more simply. How does this desire relate to the concerns of this petition?

3. Some of the early Christian writers quoted in this chapter related the bread for which we pray with the bread of Communion and with the figurative bread of the word of God. Is this helpful for you

today? How are you fed in Communion, and how does the word of God feed you?

4. Have you paid much attention to the word *daily*? What does this have to do with what Jesus says about not being overly concerned for the future? In voicing this petition, are you also committing yourself to place your future in the hands of God? Or are you simply saying, "In case I fail and cannot get my own bread, please come to my aid"?

5. Think again about the word *our* discussed in the first chapter. When we ask for "our daily bread," are we asking for bread only for us, the ones who are praying, or are we also praying in the name of those who really have no bread? How does this relate to issues of economic justice?

Chapter 8

1. The petition "Forgive us our debts, as we forgive our debtors" is also a confession. We are confessing our debt before God. If the Lord's Prayer is to be a model for all our prayer, we must each ask, What place does confession have in my devotional life, both private and corporate? Do the worship services that I attend regularly include a prayer of confession? If not, is this something important that is lacking, or is it simply an optional matter? Is there a relationship between the depth of the sin I confess and the heights of joy I experience upon being forgiven?

2. Can you name some moments when you have really felt the joy of being forgiven by God? Can you name some moments when you have really felt the joy of being forgiven by others? Have you ever felt the joy of forgiving others?

3. Different English translations of the Bible use words such as *debts*, *trespasses*, and *sins* in this petition. What value do you see in each of these translations and what shortcomings?

4. What do we mean by our "debtors" or "those who trespass against us"? Think of some examples or name them. How can you experience the joy of forgiving? Can you forgive those who have wronged you but show no remorse?

5. When you refuse to forgive another, does this harm that person? Does this harm you?

Chapter 9

1. What are the most common temptations in our day? When you are tempted, do you attribute this to your self, to the work of the Evil One, or to God? Is there a difference between tempting and testing? Is there any temptation that is not also a test? Are there tests that are not temptations?

2. What role do you see in the creation of habits and of a discipline of life as a way to resist temptation? What is the relationship between knowing the will of God and developing good habits? What resources do we have for knowing the will of God?

3. Review the entire Lord's Prayer, trying to see what phrases refer to particular temptations that you face daily. For instance, when we say "give us this day our daily bread," are we also asking God to keep us away from the temptations of greed and excessive consumption?

Chapter 10

1. From what evils are you asking to be delivered when you say this prayer? Is it legitimate, when you pray these words, to think in terms of illness, death, health, poverty, and so on? Or are you speaking only of spiritual evil and final damnation? If you lived in a country where there is persecution of Christians, what would this petition mean for you? If you were oppressed by injustice, what would it mean? When we say "Our Father," are we also praying on behalf of those living under such conditions?

2. If the words of the prayer "but deliver us from evil" are translated not as "deliver us" but rather as "free us" or as "liberate us," what does this imply for how we understand our subjection to evil and the liberating power of our Savior? We often speak of sin as a form of slavery. If it is, what are we asking for in this prayer? Are we asking simply not to have evil befall us, or are we also asking for the destruction of the power of evil that holds us captive?

3. Once again, think about the wider reach of the word *us*. I am not asking my God to deliver just me from evil. Where do you see the powers of evil holding others in subjection? Unbelief? Addictions? Abuse? Injustice?

Chapters 11 and 12

1. Pages 155–57 make a comparison between Calvin's interpretation of this prayer's final doxology and Chrysostom's. Which of these interpretations relates more closely to your experience and that of your church?

2. In churches today, this final phrase of the Lord's Prayer is used in two basic ways. In some churches, the Lord's Prayer itself is said at the end of a series of other prayers, mostly prayers of intercession. In this case, this final phrase is simply recited as part of the Lord's Prayer. In other churches, the Lord's Prayer, except this last phrase, is said before other prayers, after which the period of prayer ends with the words "for thine is the Kingdom. . . ." What difference does this make? What do you think each of these two practices emphasizes? If you were to stop at this point and add your own petitions to this prayer, what would they be?

3. This final phrase of the Lord's Prayer begins with the word *for*, which means "because." To what do you think this refers? Does it refer only to the last petition, about being delivered from evil, or does it refer to the entire prayer, which we raise because the kingdom, the power, and the glory belong to God?

4. When you pray, either in private or in the fellowship of the church, do you really understand the power of the word *Amen*? Or is it simply a way of ending prayer, a sort of "that's all for the time being"?

5. End your study by slowly repeating each of the phrases in the Lord's Prayer and taking the time to consider once again what each one means.

And may God bless you! Amen!

Notes

The following abbreviations are used in the notes:

ANF   *Ante-Nicene Fathers*

BAC   Biblioteca de autores cristianos

LW   *Luther's Works* (St. Louis: Concordia Publishing House, 1955–1986)

NPNF¹   *Nicene and Post-Nicene Fathers*, Series 1

PG   Patrologia Graeca [= Patrologiae Cursus Completus: Series Graeca], ed. Jacques-Paul Migne, 162 vols. (Paris, 1857–1886)

PL   Patrologia Latina (= Patrologiae Cursus Completus: Series Latina), ed. Jacques-Paul Migne, 217 vols. (Paris, 1844–1864)

Introduction

1. *Didache* 8.2.
2. Cyprian, *The Lord's Prayer* 2–3 (*ANF* 5.448).
3. Martin Luther, *The Sermon on the Mount*, Matthew 6:7–13 (*LW* 21.146).
4. Augustine, *Epistle* 130, *To Proba* 22.
5. Thomas Aquinas, *Summa Theologica*, 2–2, q. 83, a. 9.
6. Gregory of Nyssa, *Homilies on the Lord's Prayer* 1 (PG 44.1123).

Uses of the Prayer in the Early Church

1. Pliny the Younger, *Epistle* 96.7.

2. Tertullian, *On Prayer* 25 (*ANF* 3.690).

3. Tertullian, *On Prayer* 10 (*ANF* 3.684).

4. Hippolytus, *The Apostolic Tradition of Hippolytus* 35–36, trans. and ed. Burton Scott Easton (Cambridge: The University Press, 1934), 54–55.

5. Benedict, *Rule* 16.

6. Augustine, *Sermon* 57.1.

7. Tertullian, *On Prayer* 1 (*ANF* 3.681).

8. Cyprian, *The Lord's Prayer* 9 (*ANF* 5.449).

9. Origen, *On Prayer* 25 (PG 11.484).

Chapter 1

1. Cyprian, *The Lord's Prayer* 8 (*ANF* 5.449).

2. Theodore of Mopsuestia, *Commentary on the Lord's Prayer* 1, http://www.tertullian.org/fathers/theodore_of_mopsuestia_lordsprayer _02_text.htm.

3. John Chrysostom, *Homilies on the Gospel of Matthew* 19.6 (*NPNF¹* 10.134).

4. Justin, *First Apology* 65 (*ANF* 1.185).

5. Hippolytus, *Apostolic Tradition* 22.

Chapter 2

1. Cyprian, *On the Lord's Prayer* 10 (*ANF* 5.450).

2. Augustine, *On the Sermon on the Mount* 2.4.15.

3. Tertullian, *On Prayer* 2 (*ANF* 3.682).

4. Tertullian, *On Prayer* 2.

5. Cyprian, *On the Lord's Prayer* 11 (*ANF* 5.450).

6. Ambrose of Milan, *On the Sacraments* 5.4 (PL 16.450–51).

7. Cyprian, *On the Lord's Prayer* 9 (*ANF* 5.449).

8. Origen, *On Prayer* 22.

9. Gregory of Nyssa, *On the Lord's Prayer* 2.
10. Augustine, *Sermon* 58.2.
11. Augustine, *On Free Will* 2.1.1.
12. Augustine, *On Free Will* 2.1.3.

Chapter 3

1. Origen, *On Prayer* 13 (PG 11.485).
2. Origen, *On Prayer* 13.
3. Augustine, *On the Sermon on the Mount* 2.5.17.
4. Karl Barth, *Dogmatics in Outline* (New York: Harper & Row, 1959), 59–61.
5. John Calvin, *Institutes of the Christian Religion* 3.20.40, ed. John T. McNeill, trans. Ford Lewis Battles (Philadelphia: Westminster, 1960), 902–3.

Chapter 4

1. Thomas Aquinas, *Summa Theologica* 2-2, q. 83, a. 9.
2. Martin Luther, *The Sermon on the Mount,* Matthew 6:7–13, (*LW* 21.146).
3. Tertullian, *On Prayer* 2 (*ANF* 3.682).
4. Cyprian, *The Lord's Prayer* 12 (*ANF* 5.450).
5. Origen, *On Prayer* 24.1–5 (PG 11.492).
6. Augustine, *On the Sermon on the Mount* 6.15.
7. Gregory of Nyssa, *Homilies on the Lord's Prayer* 3 (PG 44.1156).
8. Chrysostom, *Homilies on the Gospel of Matthew* 19.7 (*NPNF¹* 10.134).

Chapter 5

1. Gregory of Nyssa, *Homilies on the Lord's Prayer* 3 (PG 44.1156).

2. Cyprian, *The Lord's Prayer* 13 (*ANF* 5.450–51).

3. Ambrose, *On the Sacraments* 5.4.42 (PL 16.451).

4. Cyprian, *The Lord's Prayer* 13.

5. Thomas Aquinas, *Summa Theologica* 2–2, q. 83, a. 9.

6. Tertullian, *On Prayer* 5.1–4 (*ANF* 3.683).

Chapter 6

1. Tertullian, *On Prayer* 4.2 (*ANF* 3.682).

2. John Calvin, *Institutes of the Christian Religion* 3.20.43, ed. John T. McNeill, trans. Ford Lewis Battles (Philadelphia: Westminster, 1960), 906.

3. Cyprian, *The Lord's Prayer* 15 (*ANF* 5.451).

4. John Chrysostom, *Homilies on the Gospel of Matthew* 19.7 (*NPNF¹* 10.134–35).

5. Augustine, *Sermon* 58.4 (BAC 95.97).

6. Cyprian, *The Lord's Prayer* 16.

7. Gregory of Nyssa, *Homilies on the Lord's Prayer* 4 (PG 44.1165).

8. Cyprian, *The Lord's Prayer* 17.

9. Augustine, *Sermon* 58.4 (BAC 95.99).

10. Tertullian, *On Prayer* 5 (*ANF* 3.683).

11. Cyprian, *The Lord's Prayer* 14.

Chapter 7

1. Tertullian, *On Prayer* 6.2 (*ANF* 3.603).

2. Cyprian, *The Lord's Prayer* 18 (*ANF* 5.452).

3. Origen, *On Prayer* 27.1–70 (PG 11.505).

4. Augustine, *On the Sermon on the Mount* 2.7.27 (BAC 121.917–19).

5. *Didache* 4.5–8 (BAC 65.81–82).

6. Shepherd of Hermas, Vision 3.9 (*ANF* 2.16).

7. Clement of Alexandria, *Christ the Educator* 2.12 (*ANF* 1.268).

8. Basil of Caesarea, *Homily on "I Shall Destroy . . ."* 1 (PG 31.276–77).

9. John Calvin, *Institutes of the Christian Religion* 3.20.40, ed. John T. Mc-Neill, trans. Ford Lewis Battles (Philadelphia: Westminster, 1960), 910.

Chapter 8

1. Tertullian, *On Prayer* 7.1 (*ANF* 3.683–84).
2. Cyprian, *The Lord's Prayer* 22 (*ANF* 5.453).
3. Martin Luther, *The Sermon on the Mount* 6:7–13, (*LW*: 23.147).
4. Cyprian, *On Prayer* 22 (*ANF* 5.543).
5. Chrysostom, *Homilies on the Gospel of Matthew* 19.15 (*NPNF¹* 10.135).
6. Ambrose, *On the Sacraments* 5.4.27 (PL 16.404).
7. Augustine, *On the Sermon on the Mount* 8.28 (BAC 121.19).
8. Anselm, *Why God Became Human* 20 (BAC 82.807).
9. Origen, *On Prayer* 18 (PG 11.403).
10. Gregory of Nyssa, *Homilies on the Lord's Prayer* 5 (PG 44.1177–81).

Chapter 10

1. Anselm of Canterbury, *Why God Became Human* 23.

Chapter 11

1. John Chrysostom, *Homily* 19.10 (*NPNF¹* 10.137).
2. Hippolytus, *The Apostolic Tradition of Hippolytus*, trans. Burton Scott Easton (Cambridge: Cambridge University Press, 1934), 49.
3. Chrysostom, *Homily* 19.10, 137.
4. John Calvin, *Institutes of the Christian Religion* 3.40.47, ed. John T. McNeill, trans. Ford Lewis Battles (Philadelphia: Westminster, 1960), 915.
5. Calvin, *Institutes* 3.40.47, 915–16.
6. Chrysostom, *Homily* 19.10, 137.

Index of Authors and Subjects

Index of Scripture